101
best
campsites
for **you & your dog**

alan
rogers

Compiled by: **Alan Rogers Guides Ltd**

Designed by: **Vine Design Ltd**

© Alan Rogers Guides Ltd 2010

Published by: **Alan Rogers Guides Ltd,**
Spelmonden Old Oast, Goudhurst, Kent TN17 1HE
www.alanrogers.com
Tel: 01580 214000

British Library Cataloguing-in-Publication Data:
A catalogue record for this book is available from
the British Library.

ISBN 978-1-906215-38-5

Printed in Great Britain by
Stephens & George Print Group

contents

Welcome to the Alan Rogers
'101' **guides**

The Alan Rogers guides have been helping campers and caravanners make informed decisions about their holiday destinations since 1968. Today, whether online or in print, Alan Rogers still provides an independent, impartial view, with detailed reports, on each campsite.

With so much unfiltered, unqualified information freely available, the Alan Rogers perspective is invaluable to make sure you make the right choice for your holiday.

What is the '101' **series**?

At Alan Rogers, we know that readers have many and diverse interests, hobbies and particular requirements. And we know that our guides, featuring a total of some 3,000 campsites, can provide a bewildering choice from which it can be difficult to produce a shortlist of possible holiday destinations.

The Alan Rogers 101 guides are devised as a means of presenting a realistic, digestible number of great campsites, featured because of their suitability to a given theme.

This book remains first and foremost an authoritative guide to excellent campsites which go out of their way to make dogs welcome and make holidaying with your dog just a little easier.

101 **Best campsites for you and your dog**

Campsites have wide-ranging policies and rules on dogs and this can sometimes be confusing.

However, the good news for those heading abroad, is that taking your dog with you has become simpler and more painless as procedures have been clarified.

This guide identifies 101 great campsites that welcome dogs, both in the UK and on the continent.

They may have certain restrictions (e.g. regarding dates, breeds, sizes and so on) so you are advised to check with the campsite directly regarding your own specific plans.

There are 101 wonderful campsites in this guide, of a wide range of styles and locations, so you are sure to find your ideal holiday destination here.

Alan Rogers – in search of 'the best'

Alan Rogers himself started off with the very specific aim of providing people with the necessary information to allow them to make an informed decision about their holiday destination. Today we still do that with a range of guides that now covers Europe's best campsites in 27 countries.

We work with campsites all day, every day. We visit campsites for inspection purposes (or even just for pleasure!). We know campsites 'inside out'.

We know which campsites would suit active families; which are great for get-away-from-it-all couples; we know which campsites are planning super new pool complexes; which campsites offer a fantastic menu in their on-site restaurant; which campsites allow you to launch a small boat from their slipway; which campsites have a decent playing area for kicking a ball around; which campsites have flat, grassy pitches and which have solid hardstandings.

We also know which are good for fishing, golf, spas and outdoor activities; which are close to the beach; and which welcome dogs. These particular themes form our new '101' series.

All Alan Rogers guides (and our website) are respected for their independent, impartial and honest assessment. The reviews are prose-based, without overuse of indecipherable icons and symbols. Our simple aim is to help guide you to a campsite that matches best your requirements – often quite difficult in today's age of information overload.

What is the **best**?

The criteria we use when inspecting and selecting sites are numerous, but the most important by far is the question of good quality. People want different things from their choice of campsite, so campsite 'styles' vary dramatically: from small peaceful campsites in the heart of the countryside, to 'all singing, all dancing' sites in popular seaside resorts.

The size of the site, whether it's part of a chain or privately owned, makes no difference in terms of it being required to meet our exacting standards in respect of its quality and it being 'fit for purpose'. In other words, irrespective of the size of the site, or the number of facilities it offers, we consider and evaluate the welcome, the pitches, the sanitary facilities, the cleanliness, the general maintenance and even the location.

Expert opinions

We rely on our dedicated team of Site Assessors, all of whom are experienced campers, caravanners or motorcaravanners, to visit and recommend campsites. Each year they travel around Europe inspecting new campsites for Alan Rogers and re-inspecting the existing ones.

When planning
your **holiday...**

A holiday should always be a relaxing affair, and a campsite-based holiday particularly so. Our aim is for you to find the ideal campsite for your holiday, one that suits your requirements. All Alan Rogers guides provide a wealth of information, including some details supplied by campsite owners themselves, and the following points may help ensure that you plan a successful holiday.

Find out more

An Alan Rogers reference number (**e.g. FR12345**) is given for each campsite and can be useful for finding more information and pictures online at **www.alanrogers.com**

Simply enter this number in the 'Campsite Search' field on the Home page.

Campsite descriptions

We aim to convey an idea of its general appearance, 'feel' and features, with details of pitch numbers, electricity, hardstandings etc.

Facilities

We list specific information on the site's facilities and amenities and, where available, the dates when these facilities are open (if not for the whole season). Much of this information is as supplied to us and may be subject to change. Should any particular activity or aspect of the campsite be important to you, it is always worth discussing with the campsite before you travel.

Swimming pools

Opening dates, any charges and levels of supervision are provided where we have been notified. In some countries (notably France) there is a regulation whereby Bermuda-style shorts may not be worn in swimming pools (for health and hygiene reasons). It is worth ensuring that you do take 'proper' swimming trunks with you.

Charges

Those given are the latest provided to us, usually 2010 prices, and should be viewed as a guide only.

Toilet blocks

We assume that toilet blocks will be equipped with a reasonable number of British style WCs, washbasins and hot showers in cubicles. We also assume that there will be an identified chemical toilet disposal point, and that the campsite will provide water and waste water drainage points and bin areas. If not the case, we comment. We do mention certain features that some readers find important: washbasins in cubicles, facilities for babies, facilities for those with disabilities and motorcaravan service points.

Reservations

Necessary for high season (roughly mid-July to mid-August) in popular holiday areas (i.e. beach resorts). You can reserve many sites via our own Alan Rogers Travel Service or through other tour operators. Remember, many sites are closed all winter and you may struggle to get an answer.

Telephone numbers

All numbers assume that you are phoning from within the country in question. From the UK or Ireland, dial 00, then the country's prefix (e.g. France is 33), then the campsite number given, but dropping the first '0'.

Opening dates

Dates given are those provided to us and can alter before the start of the season. If you intend to visit shortly after a published opening date, or shortly before the closing date, it is wise to check that it will actually be open at the time required. Similarly, some sites operate a restricted service during the low season, only opening some of their facilities (e.g. swimming pools) during the main season; where we know about this, and have the relevant dates, we indicate it – again if you are at all doubtful it is wise to check.

Accommodation

Over recent years, more and more campsites have added high quality mobile homes, chalets, lodges, gites and more. Where applicable we indicate what is available and you'll find details online.

Special Offers

Some campsites have taken the opportunity to highlight a special offer. This is arranged by them and for clarification please contact the campsite direct.

Dog days
of **summer**

Camping holidays offer a wonderful opportunity to enjoy some real 'r and r' without leaving your beloved dog behind; a change of scene, different routines, lots of fresh air will benefit everyone, whether with two legs or four. And since 3rd July 2004, with a PETS (Pet Travel Scheme) passport, your dog can enjoy a continental camping holiday just as much as you.

Dogs **on campsites**

Campsites are all about enjoying the freedom of the fresh air, wonderful scenery and a relaxed lifestyle, away from the usual routines of home. Of course, dogs can benefit from all this too! In addition they enjoy new walks, new smells and the affectionate attention of friendly passers by. They are, however, perhaps less interested in the cultural sights!

Basic **rules & etiquette**

On the continent, dogs are generally far more welcome in shops and restaurants than in the UK. A well-behaved dog sat beside the table in a restaurant is by no means uncommon.

Of course, each site has different rules so be sure to check before you book – for example, some campsites have restrictions on breeds and sizes of dog permitted. But no matter how well trained and obedient they may be, certain basic rules generally apply.

- Expect to be required to keep your dog on a lead
- Respect others
  (it may be hard to imagine, but some people do not like or are afraid of dogs)
- Don't fall out with the campsite owner, keep barking to a minimum
- Be sure to clean up after your dog

In return, you will find on many dog-friendly sites certain measures are in place to make a dog's life that little bit more pleasurable. You may find a special area set aside for exercising dogs, or perhaps a path where an evening stroll becomes a pleasant after-dinner ritual. Provision of washing stations, or dog showers, are not unheard of and even on-site dog classes have been known.

Taking your
dog **abroad**

Overheating in dogs

Travelling long distances in hot summer conditions can be dangerous for dogs. Dogs control body temperature mainly by panting. In fact, signs to look out for are abnormally heavy panting, agitated activity and perhaps whining. The dog may produce more drooling saliva than normal, and eyes may become glassy. Treat overheating promptly: find a cool shaded place, offer drinking water and spray the dog with cool water.

The pet **passport**

Of course with so many great campsites to choose from across Europe, you may be planning to head abroad. The PETS scheme is designed to stop the spread of rabies and other diseases while still allowing pets to travel between EU countries without the need for quarantine. To be eligible, your dog must:

- Be fitted with a microchip *(to assist identification on a national database)*

- Be vaccinated against rabies

- Wait 21 days from the date of their first rabies vaccination before travelling to another European Community country

In addition, your dog must be blood tested (to ensure satisfactory effect of the rabies vaccination), and must wait 6 months from the date of the blood test before re-entering the UK.

Your dog will need to be issued with a pet passport by a vet and be treated for tapeworm and ticks, not less than 24 hours and not more than 48 hours before returning to the UK. The vet will stamp the pet passport and record the time and date of treatment. Travel must be with a PETS-approved carrier for the journey back to the UK.

Forward planning is crucial – best start at least 8 months before you plan to travel.

What will it cost me?

Exact costs will vary but you can expect to pay between £120 and £160 per dog (including microchipping, rabies jab, blood test, issuing of pet passport). A vet's fee in France might cost around £20, excluding treatments. Ferry companies usually charge £10-£20 each way to take your dog.

It's a
dog's **life**

Fit to **travel**

Some tips to help make your dog's journey as comfortable as possible:

- Provide a light meal about two hours before they travel

- Allow your dog the chance to go to the toilet before setting off

- If travelling in a container, allow your dog to familiarise itself with it in advance

- Bring a familiar-smelling cushion or rug to help your dog settle

- Obvious, perhaps, but plenty of ventilation, shade and fresh drinking water are essential

- It is worth checking the regulations for the country you are visiting as some countries insist that dogs wear canine seat belts or be carried in a cage

- Make sure your dog wears an identification collar and tag with your current contact details

On the **ferry**

If crossing the Channel expect your dog to remain in the vehicle on short crossings. On longer crossings dogs may be moved to on board kennels, with provision for accompanied visits. For first time or nervous dogs, you may wish to cross the Channel with Eurotunnel, allowing you to travel with your dog in the vehicle.

Ferry tips

- Check in early – makes for a relaxed check in

- Choose a short crossing
  (e.g. to Calais or Dunkirk)

- Consider travelling overnight, when the temperature is cooler

- When boarding, ensure the officials know that you have a dog in the vehicle

- When leaving your vehicle, make sure that your dog has adequate ventilation

- Make sure your dog has drinking water

Enjoy...!

Whether you're an 'old hand' or are contemplating your first trip, a regular reader of our Guides or a new 'convert', we wish you well in your travels and hope we have been able to help in some way. We are, of course, also out and about ourselves, visiting sites, talking to owners and readers, and generally checking on standards and new developments. We hope to bump into you!

Wishing you thoroughly enjoyable camping and caravanning in 2011 – favoured by good weather of course!

The Alan Rogers Team

Further **information**

Pet Insurance

You wouldn't travel without insurance for yourself so a good pet insurance policy that covers your dog while you're away offers peace of mind.

Assistance Dogs

If travelling with an assistance dog, consult Defra and your ferry company.

Useful Websites

This is primarily a guide to excellent dog friendly campsites and does not set out to be a definitive explanation of your legal obligations. Please check your own requirements well in advance.

www.defra.gov.uk – *follow the link for travelling with pets*

www.bva.co.uk – *British Veterinary Association*

www.dogsaway.co.uk – *Vastly experienced specialists in ensuring welfare and peace of mind when travelling with dogs*

www.pethealthcouncil.co.uk – *Health issues*

www.apbc.org.uk – *Association of Pet Behaviour Counsellors*

SPAIN – Sant Pere Pescador

Camping Las Dunas

Ctra San Marti - Sant Pere, E-17470 Sant Pere Pescador (Girona)
t: 972 521 717   e: info@campinglasdunas.com
alanrogers.com/ES80400   www.campinglasdunas.com

Accommodation: ☑Pitch ☑Mobile home/chalet ☐ Hotel/B&B ☐ Apartment

Las Dunas is an extremely large, impressive and well organised resort style site with many on–site activities and an ongoing programme of improvements. It has direct access to a superb sandy beach that stretches along the site for nearly a kilometre with a windsurfing school and beach bar. There is also a much used, huge swimming pool, plus a large double pool for children. Las Dunas is very large, with 1,700 individual hedged pitches (1,479 for tourers) of around 100 m² laid out on flat ground in long, regular parallel rows. All have electricity and 180 also have water and drainage. Shade is available in some parts of the site. Much effort has gone into planting palms and new trees here and the results are very attractive. The large restaurant and bar have spacious terraces overlooking the pools and you can enjoy a very pleasant, more secluded cavern style pub. A magnificent disco club is close by in a soundproof building. With free quality entertainment of all types in season and positive security arrangements, this is a great site for families with teenagers. Member of Leading Campings Group.

You might like to know

There is a special area with pitches for dog owners (dogs are not allowed in mobile homes or chalets).

☑ **Dogs welcome** (subject to conditions)
☑ **Dogs welcome all season**
☐ **Dogs welcome part season**
☐ **Breed restrictions**
   (e.g. only small dogs accepted)
☑ **Number restrictions** (max. 1 or 2 dogs)
☑ **Dog sanitary facilities**
   (e.g. waste bins, bags)
☑ **Dog showers**
☑ **On-site dog walking area**
☐ **Kennels**
☐ **Vet nearby**
   (able to help with UK Pet Passports)

Facilities: Five excellent large toilet blocks with electronic sliding glass doors (resident cleaners 07.00-21.00). Excellent facilities for youngsters, babies and disabled visitors. Laundry facilities. Motorcaravan services. Extensive supermarket, boutique and other shops. Large bar with terrace. Large restaurant. Takeaway. Ice cream parlour. Beach bar in main season. Disco club. Swimming pools. Playgrounds. Tennis. Archery. Minigolf. Sailing/windsurfing school and other watersports. Programme of sports, games, excursions and entertainment, partly in English (15/6-31/8). ATM. Safety deposit. Internet café. WiFi. Off site: Riding and boat launching 5 km. Water park 10 km. Golf 30 km. L'Escala 5 km.

Open: 19 May - 2 September.

Directions: L'Escala is northeast of Girona on the coast between Palamós and Roses. From A7/E15 autostrada take exit 5 towards L'Escala on GI 623. Turn north 2 km. before reaching L'Escala towards Sant Marti d'Ampúrias. Site well signed. GPS: 42.16098, 3.13478

Charges guide

Per person	€ 3,50 - € 5,00
child (2-10 yrs)	€ 3,00 - € 3,25
pitch	€ 14,00 - € 52,00
dog	€ 3,20 - € 4,50

Camping Aquarius

Playa s/n, E-17470 Sant Pere Pescador (Girona)
t: **972 520 003**   e: **camping@aquarius.es**
alanrogers.com/ES80500   www.aquarius.es

Accommodation: ☑Pitch ☑Mobile home/chalet ☐ Hotel/B&B ☐ Apartment

A smart and efficient family site, Aquarius has direct access to a quiet sandy beach that slopes gently and provides good bathing (the sea is shallow for quite a long way out). Watersports are popular, particularly windsurfing (a school is provided). One third of the site has good shade with a park like atmosphere. There are 435 pitches with electricity (6/16A). Markus Rupp and his wife are keen to make every visitor's experience a happy one. The site is ideal for those who really like sun and sea with a quiet situation. The family is justifiably proud of their most attractive and absolutely pristine site which they continually upgrade and improve. The fountain at the entrance, the fishponds and the water features in the restaurant are soothing and pleasing. A small stage close to the restaurant is used for live entertainment in season. The spotless beach bar complex with shaded terraces, satellite TV and evening entertainment, has marvellous views over the Bay of Roses. The Surf Center with rentals, school and shop is ideal for enthusiasts and beginners alike.

You might like to know
The site is located between fields and meadows and a long sandy beach and as it is also very close to several National Parks, exercising your dog should not be a problem. In low season dogs are free of charge.

- ☑ **Dogs welcome** *(subject to conditions)*
- ☑ **Dogs welcome all season**
- ☐ **Dogs welcome part season**
- ☐ **Breed restrictions**
  (e.g. only small dogs accepted)
- ☐ **Number restrictions** *(max. 1 or 2 dogs)*
- ☐ **Dog sanitary facilities**
  (e.g. waste bins, bags)
- ☐ **Dog showers**
- ☐ **On-site dog walking area**
- ☐ **Kennels**
- ☐ **Vet nearby**
  (able to help with UK Pet Passports)

Facilities: Attractively tiled, fully equipped, large toilet blocks provide some cabins for each sex. Excellent facilities for disabled visitors, plus baths for children. Superb new block has underfloor heating and family cabins. Laundry. Gas supplies. Motorcaravan services. Full size refrigerators. Supermarket. Pleasant restaurant and bar with terrace. Takeaway. Purpose built play centre for children (with qualified attendant), playground and separate play area for toddlers. TV room. Surf Center. Minigolf. Bicycle hire. ATM. Internet access. WiFi. Dogs are accepted in one section. (Note: no pool). Off site: Fishing and boat launching 3 km. Riding 6 km. Golf 15 km.

Open: 15 March - 5 November.

Directions: Attention: SatNavs take you a different route, but easier to drive is from AP7 exit 3 (Figueres Nord) direction Roses on C-68. At roundabout Castello d'Empuries take second right to St Pere Pescador, cross town and river bridge. From there site is well signed. GPS: 42.18092, 3.09425

Charges guide

Per person	€ 3,00 - € 4,00
child (under 12 yrs)	free - € 2,65
pitch incl. electricity	€ 8,80 - € 42,00

No credit cards.

Camping La Ballena Alegre

E-17470 Sant Pere Pescador (Girona)
t: 902 510 520   e: infb2@ballena-alegre.com
alanrogers.com/ES80600   www.ballena-alegre.com

Accommodation: ☑Pitch ☑Mobile home/chalet ☐Hotel/B&B ☐Apartment

La Ballena Alegre is partly in a lightly wooded setting, partly open, and has almost 2 km. of frontage directly onto an excellent beach of soft golden sand (which is cleaned daily). They claim that none of the 1,531 touring pitches is more than 100 m. from the beach. The grass pitches are numbered and there is a choice of size (up to 100 m²). Electrical connections (5/10A) are available in all areas and there are 378 fully serviced pitches. A recent addition is a resort village area within the site with holiday homes and its own small pool and play area. This is a great site for families. There are restaurant and bar areas beside the pleasant terraced pool complex (four pools including a pool for children). For those who wish to drink and snack late there is a pub open until 03.00. The well managed soundproofed disco is popular with youngsters. A little train ferries people along the length of the site and a road train runs to local villages. Plenty of entertainment and activities are offered, including a well managed watersports centre, with sub-aqua, windsurfing and kite surfing.

You might like to know

In high season, a number of dog friendly pitches are available, and these are the only pitches which can be used for dogs.

☑ **Dogs welcome** (subject to conditions)
☑ **Dogs welcome all season**
☐ **Dogs welcome part season**
☐ **Breed restrictions**
   (e.g. only small dogs accepted)
☑ **Number restrictions** (max. 1 or 2 dogs)
☐ **Dog sanitary facilities**
   (e.g. waste bins, bags)
☐ **Dog showers**
☐ **On-site dog walking area**
☐ **Kennels**
☐ **Vet nearby**
   (able to help with UK Pet Passports)

Facilities: Seven well maintained toilet blocks are of a very high standard. Facilities for children, babies and disabled campers. Launderette. Motorcaravan services. Supermarket. Gas supplies. 'Linen' restaurant. Self-service restaurant and bar. Takeaway. Pizzeria and beach bar in high season. Pool complex. Jacuzzi. Tennis. Watersports centre. Fitness centre. Bicycle hire. Playgrounds. Sound proofed disco. Dancing twice weekly and organised activities, sports, entertainment, etc. ATM. In high season dogs only allowed in one zone (26/6-22/8). Internet access and WiFi. Torches useful in beach areas. Off site: Go-karting nearby with bus service. Fishing 300 m. Riding 2 km.

Open: 14 May - 20 September.

Directions: From A7 Figueres - Girona autopista take exit 5 to L'Escala GI 623 for 18.5 km. At roundabout take sign to Sant Marti d'Empúries and follow site signs. GPS: 42.15323, 3.11248

Charges guide

Per unit incl. 2 persons and electricity	€ 25,00 - € 70,00
extra person	€ 3,75 - € 4,54
child (3-9 yrs)	€ 2,70 - € 3,28
dog	€ 2,25 - € 4,74

No credit cards.

SPAIN – Roda de Bará

Camping Park Playa Bará

Ctra N340 km 1183, E-43883 Roda de Bará (Tarragona)
t: **977 802 701**   e: **info@barapark.es**
alanrogers.com/ES84100   www.barapark.es

Accommodation: ☑Pitch ☑Mobile home/chalet ☐ Hotel/B&B ☐ Apartment

This is a most impressive, family owned site near the beach, which has been carefully designed and developed. On entry you find yourself in a beautifully sculptured, tree-lined drive with an accompanying aroma of pine and woodlands and the sound of waterfalls close by. Considering its size, with over 850 pitches (fully serviced), it is still a very green and relaxing site with an immense range of activities. It is well situated with a 50 m. walk to a long sandy beach via a tunnel under the railway (some noise) to a new promenade with palms and a quality beach bar and restaurant. Much care with planning and in the use of natural stone; palms, shrubs and flowering plants gives a most pleasing tropical appearance to all aspects of the site. The impressive terraced Roman-style pool complex is the central feature of the site. Pitches vary in size and are being enlarged; the older ones are terraced and well shaded with pine trees, the newer ones more open, with a variety of trees and bushes forming separators between them. All have electricity (5A) and a sink with water. Arrive early to find space in peak weeks.

You might like to know
Dogs are not allowed in rental accommodation, nor on some local beaches.

☑ **Dogs welcome** *(subject to conditions)*

☑ **Dogs welcome all season**

☐ **Dogs welcome part season**

☐ **Breed restrictions**
  (e.g. only small dogs accepted)

☑ **Number restrictions** *(max. 1 or 2 dogs)*

☐ **Dog sanitary facilities**
  (e.g. waste bins, bags)

☐ **Dog showers**

☐ **On-site dog walking area**

☐ **Kennels**

☐ **Vet nearby**
  (able to help with UK Pet Passports)

Facilities: Excellent, fully equipped toilet blocks include private cabins and facilities for children and new block for disabled visitors. Private facilities to hire. Superb launderette. Triple motorcaravan service points. Supermarket and several other shops. Full restaurant. Large bar with simpler meals and takeaway. Three other bars and pleasant bar/restaurant on beach. Swimming pools. Jacuzzi/hydro-massage. Fronton and tennis (floodlit). Junior club. Sports area. Windsurfing school. Gym. Massage. Pétanque. Minigolf. Fishing. Entertainment centre. Bicycle hire. ATM. Hairdresser. Internet room (16 terminals). WiFi. Wellness centre with heated pools. Off site: Public transport at gate. Riding 6 km. Golf 8 km.

Open: 19 March - 26 September (all amenities).

Directions: From the A7 take exit 31. Site entrance is at the 1183 km. marker on the main N340 just opposite the Arco de Bara Roman monument from which it takes its name. GPS: 41.17, 1.46833

Charges guide

Per unit incl. 2 persons and electricity	€ 17,60 - € 42,30
extra person	€ 2,00 - € 9,70

No credit cards.

SPAIN – Oliva

Euro Camping

Partida Rabdells s/n, CN332 km²10, E-46780 Oliva (Valencia)
t: 962 854 098   e: info@eurocamping-es.com
alanrogers.com/ES86120   www.eurocamping-es.com

Accommodation: ☑Pitch ☑Mobile home/chalet ☐Hotel/B&B ☐Apartment

Approached through a new urbanisation, Euro Camping is a well maintained, British-owned site. Spacious and flat, it is set amidst many high trees, mainly eucalyptus, with its own access to a fine sandy beach. From reception with its helpful English speaking staff and interesting aviary opposite, wide tarmac or paved roads lead to 315 large, gravel based pitches which are either marked or hedged (most are for touring units). The main site road leads down to a beachside restaurant with superb views and a supermarket. Although only operating from early to late evenings, pitches located away from the generator behind reception will probably prove more peaceful.

You might like to know
There is direct access from the site onto a long sandy beach where, out of high season, dogs can swim in the Mediterranean.

☑ **Dogs welcome** *(subject to conditions)*
☑ **Dogs welcome all season**
☐ **Dogs welcome part season**
☐ **Breed restrictions**
  (e.g. only small dogs accepted)
☑ **Number restrictions** *(max. 1 or 2 dogs)*
☐ **Dog sanitary facilities**
  (e.g. waste bins, bags)
☐ **Dog showers**
☐ **On-site dog walking area**
☐ **Kennels**
☑ **Vet nearby**
  (able to help with UK Pet Passports)

Facilities: One newly built and two mature sanitary blocks are well maintained. British type WCs, preset hot water in the showers. Toilet facilities for disabled campers. Facilities for babies. Washing machines and dryer. Motorcaravan services. Well stocked shop and roast chicken takeaway. Restaurant/bar. Fridge hire. WiFi. Entertainment in high season. Gas. Bicycle hire. Off site: Golf and riding 1 km. Golf and tennis 1 km. Oliva is 3 km. with restaurants, cafés and supermarkets. Large street market on Fridays. Ideal area for cycling.

Open: All year.

Directions: From the north on the AP7 take exit 61 onto N332 and drive through Oliva. From the south exit 62 and left for Oliva. Exit at km. 213 (south) or 210 (north) signed 'urbanisation'. At roundabout take fourth (last) exit. Turn right immediately before narrow bridge. Continue along wide road, bearing right at end onto Carrer de Xeraco. Site is on the left at bottom of this road. GPS: 38.905, -0.066

Charges guide

Per unit incl. 2 persons	€ 24,90 - € 41,10
extra person	€ 3,15 - € 4,50
electricity	€ 4,30 - € 6,70

Camping Marjal

Ctra N332 km 73,4, E-03140 Guardamar del Segura (Alacant)
t: **966 727 070** e: **camping@marjal.com**
alanrogers.com/ES87430 www.campingmarjal.com

Accommodation: ☑Pitch ☑Mobile home/chalet ☐ Hotel/B&B ☐ Apartment

Marjal is located beside the estuary of the Segura river, alongside the pine and eucalyptus forests of the Dunas de Guardamar natural park. The fine sandy beach can be reached through the forest (800 m). This is a new site with a huge lagoon-style pool and a superb sports complex. There are 212 pitches on this award winning site, all with water, electricity, drainage and satellite TV points. The ground is covered with crushed marble, making the pitches clean and pleasant. The impressive pool/lagoon complex (1,100 m²) has a water cascade, an island bar plus bridge, one part sectioned as a pool for children, and a jacuzzi. The extensive sports area is also impressive with qualified instructors who will customise your fitness programme whilst consulting the doctor. No effort has been spared here; the quality heated indoor pool, light-exercise room, sauna, solarium, beauty salon, fully equipped gym and changing rooms, including facilities for disabled visitors, are of the highest quality. Aerobics and physiotherapy are also on offer. All activities are discounted for campers.

You might like to know

Dogs are welcome on site (but not in rented accommodation). A daily charge of € 1.50 to € 3.20 is applied (or € 40 per month for long stay bookings).

☑ **Dogs welcome** (subject to conditions)
☑ **Dogs welcome all season**
☐ **Dogs welcome part season**
☐ **Breed restrictions**
  (e.g. only small dogs accepted)
☑ **Number restrictions** (max. 1 or 2 dogs)
☑ **Dog sanitary facilities**
  (e.g. waste bins, bags)
☑ **Dog showers**
☑ **On-site dog walking area**
☐ **Kennels**
☑ **Vet nearby**
  (able to help with UK Pet Passports)

Facilities: Three excellent heated toilet blocks have free hot water, elegant separators between sinks, spacious showers and some cabins. Each block has high quality facilities for babies and disabled campers, modern laundry and dishwashing rooms. Car wash. Well stocked supermarket. Restaurants. Bar. Large outdoor pool complex (1/6-31/10). Heated indoor pool (low season). Fitness suite. Jacuzzi. Sauna. Solarium. Aerobics and aquarobics. Play room. Minigolf. Floodlit tennis and soccer pitch. Bicycle hire. Games room. TV room. ATM. Business centre. Internet access. Off site: Beach 800 m. Riding and golf 4 km.

Open: All year.

Directions: On N332 40 km. south of Alicante, site is on the sea side between 73 and 74 km. markers. GPS: 38.10933, -0.65467

Charges guide

Per unit incl. 2 persons and electricity	€ 38,00 - € 63,00
extra person	€ 7,00 - € 9,00
child (4-12 yrs)	€ 5,00 - € 6,00
dog	€ 2,20 - € 3,20

SPAIN – La Manga del Mar Menor

Caravaning La Manga

Autovia Cartagena - La Manga Salida 11, E-30386 La Manga del Mar Menor (Murcia)
t: **902 021 352**   e: **lamanga@caravaning.es**
alanrogers.com/ES87530   www.caravaning.es

Accommodation: ☑Pitch ☑Mobile home/chalet ☐ Hotel/B&B ☐ Apartment

This is a very large, well equipped 'holiday style' site with its own beach and both indoor and outdoor pools. With a good number of typical Spanish long stay units, the length of the site is impressive (1 km) and a bicycle is very helpful for getting about. The 1,000 regularly laid out, gravel touring pitches (100 or 110 m²) are generally separated by hedges which also provide a degree of shade. Each has 10A electricity supply, water and the possibility of satellite TV reception. This site's excellent facilities are ideally suited for holidays in the winter when the weather is very pleasantly warm. La Manga is a 22 km. long narrow strip of land, bordered by the Mediterranean on one side and by the Mar Menor on the other. There are sandy bathing beaches on both sides and considerable development in terms of hotels, apartments, restaurants, night clubs, etc. in between – a little reminiscent of Miami Beach! The site is situated on the approach to 'the strip', enjoying the benefit of its own semi-private beach with impressive palm trees alongside the Mar Menor which provides shallow warm waters.

You might like to know
Pets are not allowed in rented accommodation. The Regional Nature Reserve of Calblanque offers some good walking.

☑ **Dogs welcome** (subject to conditions)
☑ **Dogs welcome all season**
☐ **Dogs welcome part season**
☐ **Breed restrictions**
   (e.g. only small dogs accepted)
☑ **Number restrictions** (max. 1 or 2 dogs)
☐ **Dog sanitary facilities**
   (e.g. waste bins, bags)
☐ **Dog showers**
☐ **On-site dog walking area**
☐ **Kennels**
☐ **Vet nearby**
   (able to help with UK Pet Passports)

Facilities: Nine clean toilet blocks of standard design, well spaced around the site, include washbasins (all with hot water). Laundry. Gas supplies. Large well stocked supermarket. Restaurant. Bar. Snack bar. Swimming pool complex (April-Sept). Indoor pool, gymnasium (April-Oct), sauna, jacuzzi and massage service. New outdoor fitness course for adults. Open air family cinema (July/Aug). Tennis. Pétanque. Minigolf. Play area. Watersports school. Internet café (also WiFi). Winter activities including Spanish classes. Pet washing area. Max. 2 dogs. Off site: Buses to Cartagena and Murcia from outside site. Golf, bicycle hire and riding 5 km.

Open: All year.

Directions: Use exit (Salida) 11 from MU312 dual carriageway towards Cabo de Palos, signed Playa Honda (site signed also). Cross road bridge and double back on yourself. Site entrance is clearly visible beside dual carriageway with many flags flying. GPS: 37.62445, -0.74442

Charges guide

Per unit incl. 2 persons and electricity	€ 19,75 - € 34,50
extra person	€ 4,00 - € 5,00
child	€ 3,50 - € 4,00
dog	€ 1,25

Camping Roche

N340 km 19,5, Carril de Pilahito, E-11140 Conil de la Frontera (Cádiz)
t: 956 442 216   e: info@campingroche.com
alanrogers.com/ES88590   www.campingroche.com

Accommodation: ☑Pitch ☑Mobile home/chalet ☐ Hotel/B&B ☐ Apartment

Camping Roche is situated in a pine forest near white sandy beaches in the lovely region of Andalucia. It is a clean, tidy and welcoming site. Little English is spoken but try your Spanish, German or French as the staff are very helpful. A family site, it offers a variety of facilities including a sports area and swimming pools. The restaurant has good food and a pleasant outlook over the pool. Games are organised for children. A recently built extension provides further pitches, a new toilet block and a tennis court. There are now 335 pitches which include 104 bungalows to rent. There are pleasant paths in the area for mountain biking and this is an ideal base for visiting the cities of Seville and Cádiz.

You might like to know

There is a bus stop outside the site entrance with three buses daily – ideal for trips to cities such as Seville and Cadiz.

☑ **Dogs welcome** (subject to conditions)
☐ **Dogs welcome all season**
☑ **Dogs welcome part season**
☐ **Breed restrictions**
   (e.g. only small dogs accepted)
☑ **Number restrictions** (max. 1 or 2 dogs)
☐ **Dog sanitary facilities**
   (e.g. waste bins, bags)
☐ **Dog showers**
☐ **On-site dog walking area**
☐ **Kennels**
☐ **Vet nearby**
   (able to help with UK Pet Passports)

Facilities: Three toilet blocks are traditional in style and provide simple, clean facilities. Washbasins have cold water only. Washing machine. Supermarket. Bar and restaurant. Swimming and paddling pools. Sports area. Tennis. Play area. Off site: Bus stops 3 times daily outside gates.

Open: All year.

Directions: From the N340 (Cádiz - Algeciras) turn off to site at km. 19.5 point. From Conil, take El Pradillo road. Keep following signs to site. From CA3208 road turn at km. 1 and site is 1.5 km. down this road on the right. GPS: 36.31089, -6.11268

Charges guide

Per unit incl. 2 persons	
and electricity	€ 33,00
extra person	€ 6,50
child	€ 5,50
dog	€ 3,75

Low season discounts.

SPAIN – Labuerda

Camping Peña Montañesa

Ctra Ainsa - Francia km 2, E-22360 Labuerda (Huesca)
t: **974 500 032** e: **info@penamontanesa.com**
alanrogers.com/ES90600 www.penamontanesa.com

Accommodation: ☑Pitch ☑Mobile home/chalet ☐ Hotel/B&B ☐ Apartment

A large site situated quite high up in the Pyrenees near the Ordesa National Park, Peña Montañesa is easily accessible from Ainsa or from France via the Bielsa Tunnel (steep sections on the French side). The site is essentially divided into three sections opening progressively throughout the season and all have shade. The 288 pitches on fairly level grass are of about 75 m² and 10A electricity is available on virtually all. Grouped near the entrance are the facilities that make the site so attractive, including a fair sized outdoor pool and a glass-covered indoor pool with jacuzzi and sauna. Here too is an attractive bar/restaurant (with an open fire) and a terrace with a supermarket and takeaway opposite. There is an entertainment programme for children (21/6-15/9 and Easter weekend) and twice weekly for adults (July/Aug). This is quite a large site which has grown very quickly and as such, it may at times be a little hard pressed, although it is very well run. The site is ideally situated for exploring the beautiful Pyrenees. The complete town of Ainsa is listed as a national monument of Spain.

Facilities: A newer toilet block, heated when necessary, has free hot showers but cold water to open plan washbasins. Facilities for disabled visitors. Small baby room. An older block in the original area has similar provision. Washing machine and dryer. Bar, restaurant, takeaway and supermarket (all 1/1-31/12). Outdoor swimming pool (1/4-31/10). Indoor pool (all year). Playground. Boules. Bicycle hire. Riding. Rafting. Only gas barbecues are permitted. Torches required in some areas. Off site: Fishing 100 m. Skiing in season. Canoeing near.

Open: All year.

Directions: Site is 2 km. from Ainsa, on the road from Ainsa to France. GPS: 42.4352, 0.13618

Charges guide

Per unit incl. 2 persons and electricity	€ 24,60 - € 33,30

You might like to know

Camping Peña Montañesa is situated near the entrance of the National Park of Ordesa and Monte Perdido. It is a comfortable site with easy access to dramatic Pyrenean countryside.

☑ **Dogs welcome** *(subject to conditions)*

☑ **Dogs welcome all season**

☐ **Dogs welcome part season**

☐ **Breed restrictions**
(e.g. only small dogs accepted)

☑ **Number restrictions** *(max. 1 or 2 dogs)*

☐ **Dog sanitary facilities**
(e.g. waste bins, bags)

☐ **Dog showers**

☐ **On-site dog walking area**

☐ **Kennels**

☐ **Vet nearby**
(able to help with UK Pet Passports)

PORTUGAL – Caminha

Orbitur Camping Caminha

EN13 km 90, Mata do Camarido, P-4910-180 Caminha (Viana do Costelo)
t: **258 921 295** e: info@orbitur.pt
alanrogers.com/PO8010 www.orbitur.pt

Accommodation: ☑Pitch ☑Mobile home/chalet ☐ Hotel/B&B ☐ Apartment

In northern Portugal, close to the Spanish border, this pleasant site is just 200 metres from the beach. It has an attractive and peaceful setting in woods alongside the river estuary that marks the border with Spain and on the edge of the little town of Caminha. The site is shaded by tall pines with other small trees planted to mark large, sandy pitches. The main site road is surfaced but elsewhere take care not to get trapped in soft sand. Pitching and parking can be haphazard. Static units are grouped together on one side of the site. Water points, electrical supply and lighting are good. With a pleasant, open feel about the setting, fishing is possible in the estuary, and swimming, either there or from the open, sandy beach.

You might like to know
This site is just 200 m. from the beach, with an attractive location in a pine forest on the Minho river estuary.

- ☑ **Dogs welcome** (subject to conditions)
- ☑ **Dogs welcome all season**
- ☐ **Dogs welcome part season**
- ☐ **Breed restrictions**
  (e.g. only small dogs accepted)
- ☑ **Number restrictions** (max. 1 or 2 dogs)
- ☐ **Dog sanitary facilities**
  (e.g. waste bins, bags)
- ☐ **Dog showers**
- ☐ **On-site dog walking area**
- ☐ **Kennels**
- ☐ **Vet nearby**
  (able to help with UK Pet Passports)

Facilities: The clean, well maintained toilet block has British style toilets, washbasins (cold water) and hot showers, plus beach showers, extra dishwashing and laundry sinks (cold water). Laundry. Motorcaravan services. Supermarket. Small restaurant/bar with snacks (all Easter and 1/6-15/9). Bicycle hire. Off site: Beach 200 m. Fishing 200 m. Bus service 800 m.

Open: All year.

Directions: From the north, turn off the main coast road (N13-E50) just after camping sign at end of embankment alongside estuary, 1.5 km. south of ferry. From the south on N13 turn left at Hotel Faz de Minho at start of estuary and follow for 1 km. through woods to site.
GPS: 41.86635, -8.85844

Charges guide

Per person	€ 2,50 - € 4,50
child (5-10 yrs)	€ 1,30 - € 2,50
caravan and car	€ 5,60 - € 10,20
electricity	€ 2,50 - € 3,10

26

PORTUGAL – Praia de Mira

Orbitur Camping Mira

Estrada Florestal no 1 km 2, Dunas de Mira, P-3070-792 Praia de Mira (Coimbra)
t: **231 471 234** e: info@orbitur.pt
alanrogers.com/PO8070 www.orbitur.pt

Accommodation: ☑Pitch ☑Mobile home/chalet ☐ Hotel/B&B ☐ Apartment

A small, peaceful seaside site set in pinewoods, Orbitur Camping Mira is situated to the south of Aveiro and Vagos, in a quieter and less crowded area. It fronts onto a lake at the head of the Ria de Mira, which eventually runs into the Aveiro Ria. A back gate leads directly to the sea and a wide quiet beach 300 m. away. A road runs alongside the site boundary where the restaurant complex is situated resulting in some road noise. The site has around 225 pitches on sand, which are not marked but with trees creating natural divisions. Electricity and water points are plentiful. The site provides an inexpensive restaurant, snack bar, lounge bar and TV lounge. A medium sized supermarket is well stocked, with plenty of fresh produce. The Mira Ria is fascinating, with the brightly painted, decorative 'moliceiros' (traditional fishing boats).

You might like to know
A gate at the back of the campsite opens directly onto a wide sandy beach.

☑ **Dogs welcome** *(subject to conditions)*
☑ **Dogs welcome all season**
☐ Dogs welcome part season
☐ **Breed restrictions**
  (e.g. only small dogs accepted)
☑ **Number restrictions** *(max. 1 or 2 dogs)*
☐ Dog sanitary facilities
  (e.g. waste bins, bags)
☐ Dog showers
☐ On-site dog walking area
☐ Kennels
☐ Vet nearby
  (able to help with UK Pet Passports)

Facilities: The modern toilet blocks are clean, with 14 free hot showers and washing machines. Facilities for disabled visitors. Motorcaravan services. Gas supplies. Shop. Restaurant, bar and snack bar (Easter, June-Oct). TV room. Play area. Bicycle hire. WiFi at the bar. Bungalows (7) to rent. Off site: Bus service 150 m. (summer only). Fishing 500 m. Indoor pool, lake swimming and riding at Mira 7 km.

Open: 1 January - 30 November.

Directions: Take the IP5 (A25) southwest to Aveiro then the A17 south to Figuera da Foz. Then take the N109 north to Mira and follow signs west to Praia (beach) de Mira.
GPS: 40.4533, -8.79902

Charges guide

Per person	€ 4,90
child (5-10 yrs)	€ 2,50
pitch	€ 8,60 - € 11,90
electricity	€ 2,90 - € 3,50

Orbitur Camping Gala

EN109 km 4 Gala, P-3080-458 Figueira da Foz (Coimbra)
t: **233 431 492** e: **info@orbitur.pt**
alanrogers.com/PO8090 www.orbitur.pt

Accommodation: ☑Pitch ☑Mobile home/chalet ☐ Hotel/B&B ☐ Apartment

One of the best Orbitur sites, Gala has around 450 pitches on sandy terrain under a canopy of pine trees and is well cared for. Some pitches near the road are rather noisy. One can drive or walk the 300 m. from the back of the site to a private beach; you should swim with caution when it is windy – the warden will advise. The site fills in July/August and units may be very close together, but there should be plenty of room at other times. Besides the beach, Coimbra and the nearby Roman remains are well worth visiting.

You might like to know
The Boa Viagem mountain is a natural reserve and a paradise for all nature lovers.

☑ **Dogs welcome** *(subject to conditions)*
☑ **Dogs welcome all season**
☐ **Dogs welcome part season**
☐ **Breed restrictions**
  (e.g. only small dogs accepted)
☑ **Number restrictions** *(max. 1 or 2 dogs)*
☐ **Dog sanitary facilities**
  (e.g. waste bins, bags)
☐ **Dog showers**
☐ **On-site dog walking area**
☐ **Kennels**
☐ **Vet nearby**
  (able to help with UK Pet Passports)

Facilities: The three toilet blocks have British and Turkish style toilets, individual basins (some with hot water) and free hot showers. Laundry. Motorcaravan services. Gas supplies. Supermarket and restaurant/bar with terrace. Lounge. Open-air pool (June-Sept). Playground. Tennis. TV. WiFi throughout. Doctor visits in season. Car wash area. Off site: Beach 300 m. Fishing 1 km. Bicycle hire and riding 3 km.

Open: All year.

Directions: Coming from the north, the site is 4 km. south of Figueira da Foz beyond the two rivers; turn off N109 1 km. from bridge on southern edge of Gala, look for Orbitur sign on roundabout, it is then 600 m. to site. GPS: 40.11850, -8.85683

Charges guide

Per person	€ 5,10
child (5-10 yrs)	€ 2,60
pitch	€ 10,90 - € 11,90
electricity	€ 2,90 - € 3,50

PORTUGAL – Odemira

Zmar-Eco Camping Resort

Herdade ç de Mateus E.N. 393/1, San Salvador, P-7630 Odemira (Beja)
t: 707 200 626 e: **info@zmar.eu**
alanrogers.com/PO8175 www.zmar.eu

Accommodation: ☑Pitch ☑Mobile home/chalet ☐ Hotel/B&B ☐ Apartment

Zmar is an exciting new project which should be fully open this year. The site is located near Zambujeira do Mar, on the Alentejo coast. This is a highly ambitious initiative developed along very strict environmental lines. For example, renewable resources such as locally harvested timber and recycled plastic are used wherever possible and solar energy is used whenever practicable. Public indoor spaces have no air-conditioning, but there is adequate cooling through underfloor ventilation and electric fans where possible. Pitches are of 100 m² and benefit from artificial shade. Caravans and wood-clad mobile homes are also available for rent. The swimming pool complex features a large outdoor pool and an indoor pool area with a wave machine and a 'wellness' centre. Many sporting amenities will be available around the resort's 81 hectare park. These will include a sports field, bicycle hire, tennis courts under a huge tent and a military-style climbing and abseiling adventure installation. At the time of our visit many hundreds of olive trees were being planted all over the site.

You might like to know
Zmar-Eco Campo Resort & Spa was developed according to strict environmental criteria, primarily using renewable resources such as locally sourced wood and stone.

☑ **Dogs welcome** (subject to conditions)
☑ **Dogs welcome all season**
☐ **Dogs welcome part season**
☐ **Breed restrictions**
  (e.g. only small dogs accepted)
☐ **Number restrictions** (max. 1 or 2 dogs)
☐ **Dog sanitary facilities**
  (e.g. waste bins, bags)
☐ **Dog showers**
☐ **On-site dog walking area**
☐ **Kennels**
☐ **Vet nearby**
  (able to help with UK Pet Passports)

Facilities: Eight toilet blocks provide comprehensive facilities including for children and disabled visitors. Bar. Restaurant. Crêperie. Takeaway food. Large supermarket. Swimming pool. Covered pool. Wellness centre. Sports field. Games room. Play area, farm and play house. Tennis. Bicycle hire. Activity and entertainment programme. Mobile homes and caravans for rent. Caravan repair and servicing. The site's own debit card system is used for payment at all facilities. Off site: Vicentina coast and the Alentejo natural park. Sines (birthplace of Vasco de Gama). Cycle and walking tracks. Sea fishing.

Open: All year.

Directions: From the N120 from Odemira to Lagos, at roundabout in the centre of Portas de Transval turn towards Milfontes. Take turn to Cabo Sardo and then Zambujeira do Mar. Site is on the left. GPS: 37.60422, -8.73142

Charges guide

Per unit incl. 1-4 persons and electricity	€ 20,00 - € 50,00
extra person	€ 5,00 - € 10,00
child (4-12 yrs)	€ 5,00

Camping Turiscampo

N125, Espiche, Luz, P-8600 Lagos (Faro)
t: **282 789 265** e: **info@turiscampo.com**
alanrogers.com/PO8202 www.turiscampo.com

Accommodation: ☑Pitch ☑Mobile home/chalet ☐ Hotel/B&B ☐ Apartment

This good quality site has been thoughtfully refurbished and updated since it was purchased by the friendly Coll family, who are known to us from their previous Spanish site. The site provides 347 pitches for touring units, mainly in rows of terraces, all with electricity and some with shade. They vary in size (70-120 m²). The upper areas of the site are mainly used for bungalow accommodation (and are generally separate from the touring areas). A new, elevated Californian style pool plus a children's pool have been constructed. The supporting structure is a clever water cascade and surround and there is a large sun lounger area on astroturf. One side of the pool area is open to the road. The restaurant/bar has been tastefully refurbished and Roberto and staff are delighted to use their excellent English, providing good fare at most reasonable prices. The restaurant has two patios, one of which is used for live entertainment and discos in season and the other for dining out. The sea is 2 km. and the city of Lagos 4 km. with all the attractions of the Algarve within easy reach.

You might like to know
Lagos was capital of the kingdom of the Algarve from the 16th to the 18th centuries and remains a great seafaring port.

☑ **Dogs welcome** *(subject to conditions)*
☑ **Dogs welcome all season**
☐ **Dogs welcome part season**
☐ **Breed restrictions**
    (e.g. only small dogs accepted)
☑ **Number restrictions** *(max. 1 or 2 dogs)*
☐ **Dog sanitary facilities**
    (e.g. waste bins, bags)
☐ **Dog showers**
☐ **On-site dog walking area**
☐ **Kennels**
☐ **Vet nearby**
    (able to help with UK Pet Passports)

Facilities: Four toilet blocks are well located around the site. Two have been refurbished, two are new and contain modern facilities for disabled campers. Hot water throughout. Facilities for children. Washing machines. Shop. Gas supplies. Restaurant/bar. Swimming pool (March-Oct) with two terraces. Bicycle hire. Entertainment in high season on the bar terrace. Playground on sand. Adult art workshops. Aqua gymnastics. Miniclub (5-12 yrs) in season. Boules. Archery. Sports field. Cable TV. Internet. WiFi on payment. Bungalows to rent. Off site: Bus to Lagos and other towns from Praia da Luz village 1.5 km. Fishing and beach 2 km. Golf 4 km. Sailing 5 km. Boat launching 5 km. Riding 10 km.

Open: All year.

Directions: Take exit 1 from the N125 Lagos - Vila do Bispo. The impressive entrance is about 3 km. on the right. GPS: 37.10111, -8.73278

Charges guide

Per person	€ 3,10 - € 6,20
child (3-10 yrs)	€ 1,70 - € 3,10
pitch	€ 5,90 - € 13,70
electricity (6/10A)	€ 3,00 - € 4,00
dog	€ 1,00 - € 1,50

Orbitur Camping Sagres

Cerro das Moitas, P-8650-998 Sagres (Faro)
t: 282 624 371   e: info@orbitur.pt
alanrogers.com/PO8430   www.orbitur.pt

Accommodation: ☑Pitch ☑Mobile home/chalet ☐ Hotel/B&B ☐ Apartment

Camping Sagres is a pleasant site at the western tip of the Algarve, not very far from a lighthouse in the relatively unspoilt southwest corner of Portugal. With 960 pitches for tents and 120 for tourers, the sandy pitches, some terraced, are located amongst pine trees that give good shade. There are some hardstandings for motorhomes and electricity throughout. The fairly bland restaurant, bar and café/grill provide a range of reasonably priced meals. This is a reasonable site for those seeking winter sun, or as a base for exploring this 'Land's End' region of Portugal. It is away from the hustle and bustle of the more crowded resorts. The beaches and the town of Sagres (the departure point of the Portuguese navigators) with its fort, are a short drive.

You might like to know
The first Portuguese caravelas to discover the new world set sail from Sagres.

☑ **Dogs welcome** (subject to conditions)
☑ **Dogs welcome all season**
☐ **Dogs welcome part season**
☐ **Breed restrictions**
    (e.g. only small dogs accepted)
☑ **Number restrictions** (max. 1 or 2 dogs)
☐ **Dog sanitary facilities**
    (e.g. waste bins, bags)
☐ **Dog showers**
☐ **On-site dog walking area**
☐ **Kennels**
☐ **Vet nearby**
    (able to help with UK Pet Passports)

Facilities: Three spacious toilet blocks are showing some signs of wear but provide hot and cold showers and washbasins with cold water. Washing machines. Motorcaravan services. Supermarket. Restaurant/bar and café/grill (all Easter and June-Oct). TV room. Satellite TV in restaurant. Bicycle hire. Barbecue area. Playground. Fishing. Medical post. Car wash. WiFi (free). Off site: Buses from village 1 km. Beach and fishing 2 km. Boat launching 8 km. Golf 12 km.

Open: All year.

Directions: From Sagres, turn off the N268 road west onto the EN268. After about 2 km. the site is signed off to the right.
GPS: 37.02278, -8.94583

Charges guide

Per person	€ 4,90
child (5-10 yrs)	€ 2,50
caravan and car	€ 9,90 - € 10,90
electricity (6A)	€ 2,90 - € 3,50

Off season discounts (up to 70%).

ITALY – Bibione

Villaggio Turistico Internazionale

Via Colonie 2, I-30020 Bibione (Veneto)
t: **043 144 2611** e: **info@vti.it**
alanrogers.com/IT60140 www.vti.it

Accommodation: ☑Pitch ☑Mobile home/chalet ☐ Hotel/B&B ☑Apartment

This is a large, professionally run tourist village which offers all a holidaymaker could want. The Granzotto family have owned the site since the sixties and the results of their continuous improvements are impressive. There are 350 clean pitches, many fully serviced, shaded by mature trees and mostly on flat ground. The site's large sandy beach is excellent (umbrellas and loungers available for a small charge), as are all the facilities within the campsite where English speaking, uniformed assistants will help when you arrive. The tourist village is split by a main road with the main restaurant, cinema and children's club on the very smart chalet side. The professional hairdressing salon sets the luxury tone of the site. A comprehensive entertainment programme is on offer daily and the large pool provides a great flume and slides and a separate fun and spa pool. The local area is a major tourist resort but for more relaxation try the famous thermal baths at Bibione!

You might like to know
Dogs are welcome throughout this site except for the aqua park and on the beach. Dogs are welcome in some mobile homes and chalets. However, 1 km. from the site, there is a dog-friendly beach – Pluto Beach, where there is even a special dog bath.

☑ **Dogs welcome** *(subject to conditions)*

☑ **Dogs welcome all season**

☐ **Dogs welcome part season**

☐ **Breed restrictions**
(e.g. only small dogs accepted)

☐ **Number restrictions** *(max. 1 or 2 dogs)*

☑ **Dog sanitary facilities**
(e.g. waste bins, bags)

☑ **Dog showers**

☑ **On-site dog walking area**

☐ **Kennels**

☑ **Vet nearby**
(able to help with UK Pet Passports)

Facilities: Renovated apartments. Four modern toilet blocks house excellent facilities with mainly British style toilets. Excellent provision for children and disabled campers. Air conditioning in all accommodation. Washing machines and dryers. Motorcaravan service point. Supermarket. Bazaar. Good restaurant with bright yellow plastic chairs. Snack bar. New pool complex. Fitness centre. Disco. TV. Cinema and theatre. Internet. Play areas. Tennis. Electronic games. Off site: Bicycle hire 1 km. Riding 3 km. Golf 6 km. Fishing.

Open: 1 April - 26 September.

Directions: Leave A4 east of Venice at Latisana exit on Latisana road. Then take road 354 towards Ligmano, after 12 km. turn right to Beuazzana and then left to Bibione. Site is well signed on entering town.
GPS: 45.6351, 13.0374

Charges guide

Per unit incl 2 persons and electricity	€ 19,00 - € 42,00
extra person	€ 5,00 - € 10,50
child (1-5 yrs)	free - € 8,00
dog	€ 7,00

Camping Vela Blu

Via Radaelli 10, I-30013 Cavallino-Treporti (Veneto)
t: **041 968 068** e: **info@velablu.it**
alanrogers.com/IT60280 www.velablu.it

Accommodation: ☑Pitch ☑Mobile home/chalet ☐ Hotel/B&B ☐ Apartment

Thoughtfully landscaped within a natural wooded coastal environment, the tall pines here give shade while attractive flowers enhance the setting and paved roads give easy access to the pitches. The 280 pitches vary in size (55-100 m²) and shape, but all have electricity (10A) and 80 have drainage. Vela Blu is a relatively new, small, family style site and a pleasant alternative to the other massive sites on Cavallino. The clean, fine sand beach runs the length of one side of the site with large stone breakwaters for fun and fishing. The beach is fenced, making it safer for children, with access via a gate and there are lifeguards in season. There are outdoor showers and footbaths. The hub of the site is the charming restaurant and brilliant play area on soft sand, both adjoining a barbecue terrace and entertainment area. A well stocked shop is also in this area. For those who enjoy a small quiet site, Vela Blu fits the bill. Venice is easy to access as is the local water park (there is no pool here as yet). The entrance can become congested in busy periods due to limited waiting space.

You might like to know
The Palio Remiero marks the beginning of summer. It's a magnificent regatta along the Pordelio Canal amidst some marvellous scenery. The twelve districts of Cavallino-Treporti challenge one another to the rhythm of oar strokes.

☑ **Dogs welcome** *(subject to conditions)*
☑ **Dogs welcome all season**
☐ **Dogs welcome part season**
☐ **Breed restrictions**
  (e.g. only small dogs accepted)
☑ **Number restrictions** *(max. 1 or 2 dogs)*
☑ **Dog sanitary facilities**
  (e.g. waste bins, bags)
☑ **Dog showers**
☑ **On-site dog walking area**
☐ **Kennels**
☐ **Vet nearby**
  (able to help with UK Pet Passports)

Facilities: Two excellent modern toilet blocks include baby rooms and good facilities for disabled visitors. An attendant is on hand to maintain high standards. Laundry facilities. Motorcaravan service point. Medical room. Shop. Bar. Gelateria. Restaurant and takeaway. Games room. Satellite TV room. Pedalos. Windsurfing. Fishing. Bicycle hire. Entertainment. Off site: Bars, restaurants and shops. Ferry to Venice. Theme parks.

Open: 19 April - 25 September.

Directions: Leave A4 Venice - Trieste motorway at exit for 'Aeroporto' and follow signs for Jésolo and Punta Sabbioni. Site is signed after village of Cavallino. GPS: 45.45681, 12.5072

Charges guide

Per person	€ 4,00 - € 8,00
child (1-10 yrs)	free - € 8,00
seniors (over 60)	€ 3,10 - € 7,00
pitch incl. all services	€ 8,50 - € 17,00

ITALY – Cavallino-Treporti

Camping Village Europa

Via Fausta 332, I-30013 Cavallino-Treporti (Veneto)
t: 041 968 069 e: info@campingeuropa.com
alanrogers.com/IT60410 www.campingeuropa.com

Accommodation: ☑Pitch ☑Mobile home/chalet ☐ Hotel/B&B ☐ Apartment

Europa has a great position with direct access to a fine sandy beach with lifeguards. There are 411 touring pitches, all with 8A electricity, some with water, drainage and satellite TV connections. There is a separate area for campers with dogs and some smaller pitches are available for those with tents. The site is kept beautifully clean and neat and there is an impressive array of restaurants, bars, shops and leisure amenities. These are cleverly laid out along an avenue and include a jewellers, a doctor's surgery, internet services and much more. Leisure facilities are arranged around the site. A professional team provides entertainment and regular themed 'summer parties'. Some restaurant tables have pleasant sea views. Venice is easily accessible by bus and then ferry from Punta Sabbioni.

You might like to know
The Cavallino coast is a peaceful and green peninsula facing north towards the open sea, and south towards the Venetian lagoon.

☑ **Dogs welcome** (subject to conditions)
☑ **Dogs welcome all season**
☐ **Dogs welcome part season**
☐ **Breed restrictions**
   (e.g. only small dogs accepted)
☑ **Number restrictions** (max. 1 or 2 dogs)
☑ **Dog sanitary facilities**
   (e.g. waste bins, bags)
☑ **Dog showers**
☐ **On-site dog walking area**
☐ **Kennels**
☐ **Vet nearby**
   (able to help with UK Pet Passports)

Facilities: Three superb toilet blocks are kept pristine and have hot water throughout. Facilities for disabled visitors. Washing machines. Large supermarket and shopping centre. Bars, restaurants, cafés and pizzeria. New 'aqua park' with slide and spa centre. Tennis. Games room. Playground. Children's clubs. Entertainment programme. Internet access. Direct access to the beach. Windsurf and pedalo hire. Mobile homes and chalets for rent. Off site: Riding and boat launching 1 km. Golf and fishing 2 km. ATM 500 m. Walking and cycling trails. Excursions to Venice.

Open: 4 April - 30 September.

Directions: From A4 autostrada (approaching from Milan) take Mestre exit and follow signs initially for Venice airport and then Jésolo. From Jésolo, follow signs to Cavallino from where site is well signed. GPS: 45.47380, 12.54903

Charges guide

Per person	€ 4,00 - € 7,90
child (2-5 yrs)	€ 3,00 - € 6,90
adult over 60 yrs	€ 3,40 - € 7,80
pitch	€ 8,20 - € 20,50
dog	€ 2,00 - € 4,50

No credit cards.

ITALY – Punta Sabbioni

Camping Marina di Venezia

Via Montello 6, I-30013 Punta Sabbioni (Veneto)
t: 041 530 2511   e: camping@marinadivenezia.it
alanrogers.com/IT60450   www.marinadivenezia.it

Accommodation: ☑Pitch ☑Mobile home/chalet ☐ Hotel/B&B ☐ Apartment

This is a very large site (2,862 pitches) with much the same atmosphere as many other large sites along this appealing stretch of coastline. Marina di Venezia, however, has the advantage of being within walking distance of the ferry to Venice. It will appeal particularly to those who enjoy an extensive range of entertainment and activities, and a lively atmosphere. Individual pitches are marked out on sandy ground, most separated by trees or hedges. They are of an average size for the region (around 80 m²) and all are equipped with electricity and water. The site's excellent sandy beach is one of the widest along this stretch of coast and has a pleasant beach bar. The main pool is Olympic size and there is also a very large children's pool adjacent. The magnificent Aqua Marina Park swimming pool complex is now open and offers amazing amenities (free to all campers). This is a well run site with committed management and staff.

You might like to know
Dogs are not permitted to join you on the beach. Dogs must always be kept on a lead.

☑ **Dogs welcome** *(subject to conditions)*
☑ **Dogs welcome all season**
☐ **Dogs welcome part season**
☐ **Breed restrictions**
   (e.g. only small dogs accepted)
☐ **Max. 2 dogs per pitch**
☑ **Dog sanitary facilities**
   (e.g. waste bins, bags)
☑ **Dog showers**
☑ **On-site dog walking area**
☐ **Kennels**
☑ **Vet nearby**
   (able to help with UK Pet Passports)

Facilities: Ten modern toilet blocks are maintained to a high standard with good hot showers and a reasonable proportion of British style toilets. Good provision for disabled visitors. Washing machines and dryers. Range of shops. Several bars, restaurants and takeaways. Swimming pool complex with slides and flumes. Several play areas. Tennis. Windsurf and catamaran hire. Kite hire. Wide range of organised entertainment. WiFi internet access in all bars and cafés. Church. Special area and facilities for dog owners.

Open: 25 April - 30 September.

Directions: From A4 motorway, take Jésolo exit. After Jésolo continue towards Punta Sabbioni. Site is clearly signed to the left towards the end of this road, close to the Venice ferries. GPS: 45.43750, 12.43805

Charges guide

Per unit incl. 2 persons and electricity	€ 19,80 - € 45,20
extra person	€ 6,90 - € 9,20
child or senior (2-5 yrs and over 60)	€ 3,70 - € 7,40
dog	€ 1,10 - € 2,90

ITALY – Darè

Camping Val Rendena

Via Civico 117, I-38080 Darè (Trentino - Alto Adige)
t: **046 580 1669** e: **info@campingvalrendena.com**
alanrogers.com/IT62135 www.campingvalrendena.com

Accommodation: ☑Pitch ☑Mobile home/chalet ☐Hotel/B&B ☑Apartment

Set in the National Park of Adamello Brenta, the only natural refuge of the European brown bear, Camping Val Rendena, is an enthusiastically run family site. There are 52 level grass touring pitches with some tree shade, all with 6A electricity. The site's location makes it an ideal base from which to explore this beautiful region, rich in flora and fauna, where in summer snow still rests on peaks over 3,500 m. high. Beside the site runs the Sarca River, bordered for much of its journey by a cycle way. Surrounding the site, wooded hills with marked paths reach up to 1,800 m. In total the park has 700 km. of paths. In the friendly reception a host of very useful park information is available informing visitors of what this region, dominated by the Dolomites, has to offer. At the top of the valley is the 1,500 m. high ski resort of Madonna di Campiglio where, below the tree line, forests of larch and pine shade the endless routes for walkers, mountain bike and cycle riders. As one descends to Darè, in this region with an abundance of water, side valleys open up revealing their lakes, waterfalls and streams.

Special offers
Special low season discounts are available – please contact the site for details.

You might like to know
A dog sitting service is offered. Vet 5 km.

☑ **Dogs welcome** (subject to conditions)
☑ **Dogs welcome all season**
☐ **Dogs welcome part season**
☐ **Breed restrictions**
    (e.g. only small dogs accepted)
☑ **Number restrictions** (max. 1 or 2 dogs)
☐ **Dog sanitary facilities**
    (e.g. waste bins, bags)
☐ **Dog showers**
☑ **On-site dog walking area**
☑ **Kennels**
☑ **Vet nearby**
    (able to help with UK Pet Passports)

Facilities: Two sanitary units, a small one in the reception block, a larger one at centre of site. Free hot water, controllable showers, some washbasins in cabins. Facilities for disabled visitors. Baby room. Laundry. Motorcaravan service area. Shop selling essential items. Solar heated swimming pool with adjoining children's pool. Play area and play room. Bicycle hire. Communal barbecue. Three apartments to rent. Off site: Pizza restaurant adjoins site. Thermal baths, Golf, Tennis.

Open: 10 May - 30 September.

Directions: Site is 35 km. northwest of Trento. From the A22 (E45) Brenner - Verona autostrada take exit for Trento-Centro. Then travel westerly on the SS45b to Sarche, then SS237 to Ponte Arche and Tione di Trento. From here head north on the SS239 towards Madonna di Campiglio for about 10 km. to Darè. Entering Darè take descending slip road to the right then follow camping signs to site. GPS: 46.07077, 10.7197

Charges guide

Per unit incl. 2 persons and electricity	€ 24,60 - € 28,60
extra person	€ 7,80 - € 8,80
child (3-12 yrs)	€ 6,80 - € 7,80
dog	€ 3,00 - € 3,50

ITALY – Lévico Terme

Camping Lévico

Localitá Pleina 5, I-38056 Lévico Terme (Trentino - Alto Adige)
t: 046 170 6491   e: mail@campinglevico.com
alanrogers.com/IT62290   www.campinglevico.com

Accommodation: ☑ Pitch ☑ Mobile home/chalet ☐ Hotel/B&B ☐ Apartment

Sister site to Camping Jolly, Camping Lévico is in a natural setting on the small, very pretty Italian lake also called Lévico, which is surrounded by towering mountains. The sites are owned by two brothers – Andrea, who manages Lévico, and Gino, based at Jolly. Both campsites are charming. Lévico has some pitches along the lake edge and a quiet atmosphere. There is a shaded terrace for enjoying pizza and drinks in the evening. Pitches are of a good size, mostly grassed and well shaded with 6A electricity. Staff are welcoming and fluent in many languages including English. There is a small supermarket on site and it is a short distance to the local village. The beautiful grass shores of the lake are ideal for sunbathing and the crystal clear water is ideal for enjoying (non-motorised) water activities. This is a site where the natural beauty of an Italian lake can be enjoyed without being overwhelmed by commercial tourism. All the amenities at Camping Jolly can be enjoyed by traversing a very pretty walkway along a stream where we saw many trout.

You might like to know
Large private beach. The clear, shallow waters of the lake offer opportunities for swimming, fishing, canoeing, and boating. You can rent canoes and pedal boats from reception.

☑ **Dogs welcome** (subject to conditions)

☑ **Dogs welcome all season**

☐ **Dogs welcome part season**

☐ **Breed restrictions**
   (e.g. only small dogs accepted)

☑ **Number restrictions** (max. 1 or 2 dogs)

☑ **Dog sanitary facilities**
   (e.g. waste bins, bags)

☐ **Dog showers**

☑ **On-site dog walking area**

☐ **Kennels**

☐ **Vet nearby**
   (able to help with UK Pet Passports)

Facilities: Four modern sanitary blocks provide hot water for showers, washbasins and washing. Mostly British style toilets. Single locked unit for disabled visitors. Washing machines and dryer. Ironing. Freezer. Motorcaravan service point. Bar/restaurant, takeaway and good shop. Play area. Miniclub and entertainment (high season). Fishing. Satellite TV and cartoon cinema. Internet access. Kayak hire. Tennis. Torches useful. Off site: Town 2 km. with all the usual facilities and ATM. Bicycle hire 1.5 km. and bicycle track. Boat launching 500 m. Riding 3 km. Golf 7 km.

Open: 1 April - 11 October.

Directions: From A22 Verona - Bolzano road take turn for Trento on S47 to Lévico Terme where campsite is very well signed.
GPS: 46.00799, 11.28454

Charges guide

Per person	€ 5,00 - € 9,50
child (3-11 yrs)	€ 4,00 - € 6,00
pitch incl. electricity (6A)	€ 7,50 - € 18,00

La Rocca Camp

Localitá San Pietro, I-37011 Bardolino (Lake Garda)
t: 045 721 1111   e: info@campinglarocca.com
alanrogers.com/IT63600   www.campinglarocca.com

Accommodation: ☑Pitch ☑Mobile home/chalet ☐ Hotel/B&B ☐ Apartment

This site was one of the first to operate on the Lake and the family has a background of wine and olive oil production. La Rocca is in two areas, each side of the busy A249, the upper part being used mostly for bungalows, although some touring pitches are here and these have great lake views. The remaining touring pitches are on the lower part of the site, along with the main facilities. There is access between the two parts via a tunnel. The 450 pitches are mostly on terraces with shade, 6A electricity and access from narrow tarmac roads. This is a family site and, with the pools and direct access to the lake, provides a choice of watersports. The huge Gardaland theme park is close by (a free bus runs from the site gate). Many of the facilities have been renewed here and the owners are keen to please their guests. This site is not ideal for campers with mobility problems as there are large distances to cover to get to some facilities and the only access to the pool is by more than 30 steps, but otherwise it is a pleasant place to spend time relaxing.

Special offers
Special event 'Doggy Weekend' with professional trainers. The course is free of charge.

You might like to know
Dogs are welcome but they must be kept on a leash. They are also allowed in our Maxicaravans but not in the apartments. Two dog areas with showers are available.

☑ **Dogs welcome** (subject to conditions)

☑ **Dogs welcome all season**

☐ **Dogs welcome part season**

☐ **Breed restrictions**
   (e.g. only small dogs accepted)

☑ **Number restrictions** (max. 1 or 2 dogs)

☐ **Dog sanitary facilities**
   (e.g. waste bins, bags)

☑ **Dog showers**

☑ **On-site dog walking area**

☐ **Kennels**

☑ **Vet nearby**
   (able to help with UK Pet Passports)

Facilities: Four toilet blocks with two on each side of the site. WCs are mixed British and Turkish style and showers are controllable. Facilities for disabled visitors but many steps to pool. Children's facilities and baby baths. Washing machines. New motorcaravan services. Shop and bakery. Restaurant, bar and takeaway with large terrace. Swimming and paddling pools (lifeguard). Sun terrace with views. Pool bar. Play area. Entertainment programme in season. Miniclub. Internet point. Bicycle hire. Games room. Watersports. Torches useful. Off site: Public transport at gate. Boat launching 20 m. Riding 8 km. ATM 1.5 km.

Open: 26 March - 3 October.

Directions: Site is on the east side of Lake Garda, on the lake ring road 249. From the A4 take Pescheria exit and the 249 north for Garda (there are many signs for Gardaland). Site is well signed approaching village of Bardolino. GPS: 45.5645, 10.7129

Charges guide

Per person	€ 4,90 - € 8,90
child (0-10 yrs)	free - € 7,50
pitch	€ 8,90 - € 19,20
dog	€ 2,60 - € 5,20

CROATIA – Rovinj

Camping Polari

Polari bb, HR-52210 Rovinj (Istria)
t: 052 801 501   e: polari@maistra.hr
alanrogers.com/CR6732   www.CampingRovinjVrsar.com

Accommodation: ☑Pitch ☑Mobile home/chalet ☐Hotel/B&B ☐Apartment

This 60 hectare site has excellent facilities for both textile and naturist campers, the latter having a reserved area of 12 hectares called Punta Eva. Prime places are taken by permanent customers but there are some numbered pitches which are very good. Many of the pitches have been thoughtfully upgraded and now a new pitch (100 m²) is offered with full facilities. Pitches are clean, neat and level and there will be shade when the young trees grow. There is something for everyone here to enjoy or you may prefer just to relax. An impressive swimming pool complex is child friendly with large paddling areas. Part of the Maistia Group, the site has undergone a massive improvement programme and the result makes it a very attractive option. Enjoy a meal on the huge restaurant terrace with panoramic views of the sea.

You might like to know

The campsite is surrounded and shaded by evergreen trees making it an ideal dog exercising area.

☑ Dogs welcome *(subject to conditions)*
☑ Dogs welcome all season
☐ Dogs welcome part season
☐ Breed restrictions
   (e.g. only small dogs accepted)
☐ Number restrictions *(max. 1 or 2 dogs)*
☐ Dog sanitary facilities
   (e.g. waste bins, bags)
☑ Dog showers
☑ On-site dog walking area
☐ Kennels
☐ Vet nearby
   (able to help with UK Pet Passports)

Facilities: All the sanitary facilities have been renovated to a high standard with plenty of hot water and good showers. Washing machines and dryers. Laundry service including ironing. Motorcaravan service point. Two shops, one large and one small, one restaurant and snack bar. Tennis. Minigolf. Children's entertainment with all major European languages spoken. Bicycle hire. Watersports. Sailing school. Off site: Riding 1 km. Five buses daily to and from Rovinj (3 km). Golf 30 km.

Open: 1 April - 2 October.

Directions: From any access road to Rovinj look for red signs to AC Polari (amongst other destinations). The site is about 3 km. south of Rovinj. GPS: 45.06286, 13.67489

Charges guide

Per unit incl. 2 persons and electricity	€ 18,00 - € 40,80
extra person (18-64 yrs)	€ 5,00 - € 8,90
children and seniors according to age	free - € 8,50

For stays less than 3 nights in high season add 20%.

Camping Stoja

Stoja 37, HR-52100 Pula (Istria)
t: 052 387 144   e: acstoja@arenaturist.hr
alanrogers.com/CR6742   www.arenaturist.hr

Accommodation: ☑Pitch ☑Mobile home/chalet ☐ Hotel/B&B ☐ Apartment

Camping Stoja in Pula is an attractive and well maintained site on a small peninsula and therefore almost completely surrounded by the waters of the clear Adriatic. In the centre of the site is the old Fort Stoja, built in 1884 for coastal defence. Some of its buildings are now used as a toilet block and laundry and its courtyard is used by the entertainment team. The 708 touring pitches here vary greatly in size (50-120 m²) and are marked by round, concrete, numbered blocks, separated by young trees. About half have shade from mature trees and all are slightly sloping on grass and gravel. Pitches close to the pebble and rock beach have beautiful views of the sea and Pula. This site is an ideal base for visiting Pula, considered to be the capital of Istrian tourism and full of history, tradition and natural beauty, including a spectacular Roman amphitheatre.

You might like to know
This site enjoys an idyllic setting, surrounded by rich pine forests and Mediterranean plants, and beaches which slope into the sea.

☑ **Dogs welcome** *(subject to conditions)*
☑ **Dogs welcome all season**
☐ **Dogs welcome part season**
☐ **Breed restrictions**
  (e.g. only small dogs accepted)
☑ **Number restrictions** *(max. 1 or 2 dogs)*
☐ **Dog sanitary facilities**
  (e.g. waste bins, bags)
☐ **Dog showers**
☐ **On-site dog walking area**
☐ **Kennels**
☐ **Vet nearby**
  (able to help with UK Pet Passports)

Facilities: Five toilet blocks with British and Turkish style toilets, open plan washbasins with cold water only and controllable hot showers. Child-size basins. Facilities for disabled visitors. Laundry and ironing service. Fridge box hire. Motorcaravan service point. Supermarket. Bar/restaurant. Miniclub and teen club. Bicycle hire. Water skiing. Boat hire. Boat launching. Surfboard and pedalo hire. Fishing (with permit). Island excursions. Off site: Pula (walking distance). Riding 8 km. Golf 10 km.

Open: 4 April - 2 November.

Directions: From Pula follow site signs.
GPS: 44.85972, 13.81450

Charges guide

Per person	€ 4,30 - € 7,50
child (4-12 yrs)	€ 2,90 - € 4,70
pitch incl. electricity	€ 8,80 - € 19,10
dog	€ 2,60 - € 4,70

CROATIA – Martinscica

Camping Slatina

Martinscica, HR-51556 Cres (Kvarner)
t: 051 574 127   e: info@camp-slatina.com
alanrogers.com/CR6768   www.camps-cres-losinj.com

Accommodation: ☑Pitch ☑Mobile home/chalet ☐ Hotel/B&B ☐ Apartment

Camping Slatina lies about halfway along the island of Cres, beside the fishing port of Martinscica on a bay of the Adriatic Sea. It has 370 pitches for tourers, many with 10A electricity, 50 new individual ones (29 fully serviced) off very steep, tarmac access roads, sloping down to the sea. The pitches are large and level on a gravel base and enjoy plenty of shade from mature laurel trees, although hardly any have views. Whilst there is plenty of privacy, the site does have an enclosed feeling. Some pitches in the lower areas have water, electricity and drainage. Like so many sites in Croatia, Slatina has a private diving centre. Lastovo is surrounded by reefs and little islands and the crystal clear waters of the Adriatic make it perfect for diving. Martinscica owes its name to the medieval church of the Holy Martin and has a Glagolite monastery, standing next to the 17th century castle, built by the Patrician Sforza. Both are well worth a visit.

You might like to know
This site has been recognised by the German ADAC guide as being dog friendly.

☑ **Dogs welcome** *(subject to conditions)*
☑ **Dogs welcome all season**
☐ **Dogs welcome part season**
☐ **Breed restrictions**
   (e.g. only small dogs accepted)
☐ **Number restrictions** *(max. 1 or 2 dogs)*
☑ **Dog sanitary facilities**
   (e.g. waste bins, bags)
☑ **Dog showers**
☑ **On-site dog walking area**
☐ **Kennels**
☑ **Vet nearby**
   (able to help with UK Pet Passports)

Facilities: Four new and two refurbished toilet blocks provide toilets, open style washbasins and controllable hot showers. Facilities for disabled visitors. Laundry with sinks and washing machine. Fridge box hire. Car wash. Shop. Bar, restaurant, grill restaurant, pizzeria and fish restaurant. Playground. Minigolf. Fishing. Bicycle hire. Diving centre. Boat launching. Pedalo, canoe and boat hire. Excursions to the 'Blue Cave'. Off site: Martinscica with bars, restaurants and shops 2 km.

Open: Easter - 10 October.

Directions: From Rijeka take no. 2 road south towards Labin and take ferry to Cres at Brestova. From Cres go south towards Martinscica and follow site signs. GPS: 44.82333, 14.34083

Charges guide

Per unit incl. 2 persons, electricity and water	€ 14,21 - € 23,46
extra person	€ 4,71 - € 7,68
child (7-12 yrs)	€ 2,36 - € 3,57
dog	€ 3,00

SLOVENIA – Lesce

Camping Sobec

Sobceva cesta 25, SLO-4248 Lesce
t: 045 353 700 e: sobec@siol.net
alanrogers.com/SV4210 www.sobec.si

Accommodation: ☑ Pitch ☑ Mobile home/chalet ☐ Hotel/B&B ☐ Apartment

Sobec is situated in a valley between the Julian Alps and the Karavanke Mountains, in a pine grove between the Sava Dolinka river and a small lake. It is only 3 km. from Bled and 20 km. from the Karavanke Tunnel. There are 500 unmarked pitches on level, grassy fields off tarmac access roads (450 for touring units), all with 16A electricity. Shade is provided by mature pine trees and younger trees separate some pitches. Camping Sobec is surrounded by water – the Sava river borders it on three sides and on the fourth is a small, artificial lake with grassy fields for sunbathing. Some pitches have views over the lake, which has an enclosed area providing safe swimming for children. This site is a good base for an active holiday, since both the Sava Dolinka and the Sava Bohinjka rivers are suitable for canoeing, kayaking, rafting and fishing, whilst the nearby mountains offer challenges for mountain climbing, paragliding and canyoning.

You might like to know
The village of Lesce is 2 km. away, accessible by road or you can take the shorter path through the forest.

☑ **Dogs welcome** *(subject to conditions)*
☑ **Dogs welcome all season**
☐ **Dogs welcome part season**
☐ **Breed restrictions**
  (e.g. only small dogs accepted)
☑ **Number restrictions** *(max. 1 or 2 dogs)*
☐ **Dog sanitary facilities**
  (e.g. waste bins, bags)
☐ **Dog showers**
☐ **On-site dog walking area**
☐ **Kennels**
☐ **Vet nearby**
  (able to help with UK Pet Passports)

Facilities: Three traditional style toilet blocks (all now refurbished) with mainly British style toilets, washbasins in cabins and controllable hot showers. Child size toilets and basins. Well equipped baby room. Facilities for disabled visitors. Laundry facilities. Motorcaravan service point. Supermarket, bar/restaurant with stage for live performances. Playgrounds. Rafting, canyoning and kayaking organised. Miniclub. Tours to Bled and the Triglav National Park organised. Off site: Golf and riding 2 km.

Open: 21 April - 30 September.

Directions: Site is off the main road from Lesce to Bled and is well signed just outside Lesce. GPS: 46.35607, 14.14992

Charges guide

Per unit incl. 2 persons and electricity	€ 24,80 - € 29,00
extra person	€ 10,70 - € 12,80
child (7-14 yrs)	€ 8,00 - € 9,60
dog	€ 3,50

SLOVENIA – Recica ob Savinji

Camping Menina

Varpolje 105, SLO-3332 Recica ob Savinji
t: 035 835 027 e: info@campingmenina.com
alanrogers.com/SV4405 www.campingmenina.com

Accommodation: ☑Pitch ☑Mobile home/chalet ☐Hotel/B&B ☐Apartment

Menina Camping is in the heart of the 35 km. long Upper Savinja Valley, surrounded by 2,500 m. high mountains and unspoilt nature. It is being improved every year by the young, enthusiastic owner, Jurij Kolenc and has 200 pitches, all for touring units, on grassy fields under mature trees and with access from gravel roads. All have 6-10A electricity. The Savinja river runs along one side of the site, but if its water is too cold for swimming, the site also has a lake which can be used for swimming as well. This site is a perfect base for walking or mountain biking in the mountains. A wealth of maps and routes is available from reception. Rafting, canyoning and kayaking, or visits to a fitness studio, sauna or massage salon are organised. The site is now open all year to offer skiing holidays.

You might like to know

This is great walking country. For more experienced hikers, there are a number of peaks over 2,000 m, surrounding the Logar Valley.

☑ **Dogs welcome** *(subject to conditions)*
☑ **Dogs welcome all season**
☐ **Dogs welcome part season**
☐ **Breed restrictions**
   (e.g. only small dogs accepted)
☑ **Number restrictions** *(max. 1 or 2 dogs)*
☐ **Dog sanitary facilities**
   (e.g. waste bins, bags)
☐ **Dog showers**
☐ **On-site dog walking area**
☐ **Kennels**
☐ **Vet nearby**
   (able to help with UK Pet Passports)

Facilities: Two toilet blocks (one new) have modern fittings with toilets, open plan washbasins and controllable hot showers. Motorcaravan service point. Bar/restaurant with open air terrace (evenings only) and open air kitchen. Sauna. Playing field. Play area. Fishing. Mountain bike hire. Giant chess. Russian bowling. Excursions (52). Live music and gatherings around the camp fire. Indian village. Hostel. Skiing in winter. Kayaking. Mobile homes to rent. Off site: Fishing 2 km. Recica and other villages with much culture and folklore are close. Indian sauna at Coze.

Open: All year.

Directions: From Ljubljana take A1 towards Celje. Exit at Sentupert and turn north towards Mozirje. Follow signs Recica ob Savinj from there. Continue through Recica to Nizka and follow site signs. GPS: 46.31168, 14.90913

Charges guide

Per unit incl. 2 persons and electricity	€ 19,00 - € 22,00
extra person (over 16 yrs)	€ 8,00 - € 9,50

Camping Terme Catez

Topliska cesta 35, SLO-8251 Catez ob Savi
t: **074 936 700** e: **info@terme-catez.si**
alanrogers.com/SV4415 www.terme-catez.si

Accommodation: ☑Pitch ☑Mobile home/chalet ☐Hotel/B&B ☐Apartment

Terme Catez is part of the modern Catez thermal spa, renowned for its medical programmes to treat rheumatism and for a wide range of programmes to improve or maintain your health. The campsite has 590 pitches, with 190 places for tourers, the remainder being taken by privately owned mobile homes and cottages. One large, open field, with some young trees – a real sun trap – provides level, grass pitches which are numbered by markings on the tarmac access roads. All have 10A electricity. It would be a very useful stop over on a journey to Croatia in the low season or for an active family holiday. The site is in the centre of a large complex which caters for most needs with its pools, large shopping centre, gym and the numerous events that are organised, such as the Magic School and Junior Olympic Games for children.

You might like to know

A wide range of leisure facilities are on offer here, including several swimming pools.

☑ **Dogs welcome** *(subject to conditions)*
☑ **Dogs welcome all season**
☐ **Dogs welcome part season**
☐ **Breed restrictions**
  (e.g. only small dogs accepted)
☑ **Number restrictions** *(max. 1 or 2 dogs)*
☐ **Dog sanitary facilities**
  (e.g. waste bins, bags)
☐ **Dog showers**
☐ **On-site dog walking area**
☐ **Kennels**
☐ **Vet nearby**
  (able to help with UK Pet Passports)

Facilities: Two modern toilet blocks with British and Turkish style toilets, open style washbasins and controllable hot showers. Child size washbasins. Facilities for disabled visitors. Laundry facilities. Motorcaravan service point. Supermarket. Kiosks for fruit, newspapers, souvenirs and tobacco. Restaurants. Bar with terrace. Several large indoor and outdoor pools (free, max. two entries per day per person). Go karts. Pedaloes. Rowing boats. Jogging track. Fishing. Golf. Bicycle hire. Sauna. Solarium. Riding. Magic shows, dance nights and fashion shows organised. Casino. Video games. Off site: Golf 7 km.

Open: All year.

Directions: From Ljubljana take no. 1 road southeast towards Zagreb and follow signs for Terme Catez (close to Brezice).
GPS: 45.89137, 15.62598

Charges guide

Per person	€ 17,00 - € 21,50
child (4-12 yrs)	€ 8,50 - € 10,75
electricity	€ 4,40
dog	€ 4,00

Camping Manor Farm 1

CH-3800 Interlaken-Thunersee (Bern)
t: 033 822 2264   e: **manorfarm@swisscamps.ch**
alanrogers.com/CH9420   www.manorfarm.ch

Accommodation: ☑Pitch ☑Mobile home/chalet ☑Hotel/B&B ☐ Apartment

Manor Farm has been popular with British visitors for many years, as this is one of the traditional touring areas of Switzerland. The flat terrain is divided into 525 individual, numbered pitches which vary considerably, both in size (60-100 m²) and price with 4/13A electricity available and shade in some places. There are 144 equipped with electricity, water and drainage and 55 also have cable TV connections. Reservations are made, although you should find space except perhaps in late July/early August, but the best places may then be taken. Around 50% of the pitches are taken by permanent or letting units and a tour operator's presence. The site lies outside the town on the northern side of the Thuner See, with most of the site between road and lake but with one part on the far side of the road. Interlaken is very much a tourist town but the area is rich in scenery, with innumerable mountain excursions and walks available. The lakes and Jungfrau railway are near at hand. Manor Farm is a large campsite, efficiently run with a minimum of formality and would suit those looking for an active family holiday.

You might like to know

Manor Farm is one of Switzerland's best known sites. This south-facing campsite is surrounded by dramatic mountains with views towards the Bernese Oberland.

☑ **Dogs welcome** *(subject to conditions)*
☑ **Dogs welcome all season**
☐ **Dogs welcome part season**
☐ **Breed restrictions**
  (e.g. only small dogs accepted)
☑ **Number restrictions** *(max. 1 or 2 dogs)*
☐ **Dog sanitary facilities**
  (e.g. waste bins, bags)
☐ **Dog showers**
☐ **On-site dog walking area**
☐ **Kennels**
☐ **Vet nearby**
  (able to help with UK Pet Passports)

Facilities: Eight separate toilet blocks are practical, heated and fully equipped. Twenty private toilet units are for rent. Laundry facilities. Motorcaravan services. Gas supplies. Excellent shop (1/4-15/10). Site-owned restaurant adjoining (1/3-30/11). Snack bar with takeaway (July/Aug). TV room. Minigolf. Bicycle hire. Sailing and windsurfing school. Lake swimming. Boat hire (slipway for your own). Fishing. Daily activity and entertainment programme in high season. Excursions. Max. 1 dog. WiFi (charged). Off site: Golf 500 m. (handicap card). Riding 3 km. Free bus service to heated indoor and outdoor swimming pools (free entry).

Open: All year.

Directions: Site is 3 km. west of Interlaken along the road running north of the Thunersee towards Thun. Follow signs for 'Camp 1'. From the A8 (bypassing Interlaken) take exit 24 marked 'Gunten, Beatenberg', which is a spur road bringing you out close to site.
GPS: 46.68509, 7.81222

Charges guide

Per unit incl. 2 persons and electricity	CHF 37,00 - 63,50
extra person	CHF 10,50
child (6-15 yrs)	CHF 5,00
dog	CHF 4,00

SWITZERLAND – Interlaken

Camping Lazy Rancho 4

Lehnweg 6, CH-3800 Interlaken (Bern)
t: 033 822 8716　e: info@lazyrancho.ch
alanrogers.com/CH9430　www.lazyrancho.ch

Accommodation: ☑Pitch ☑Mobile home/chalet ☐Hotel/B&B ☐Apartment

This super site is in a quiet location with fantastic views of the dramatic mountains of Eiger, Monch and Jungfrau. Neat, orderly and well maintained, the site is situated in a wide valley just 1 km. from Lake Thun and 1.5 km. from Interlaken. The English speaking owners lovingly care for the site and will endeavour to make you feel very welcome. Connected by gravel roads, the 155 pitches, of which 90 are for touring units, are on well tended level grass (some with hardstanding, all with 10A electricity). Twenty eight pitches also have water and waste water drainage. This is a quiet friendly site, popular with British visitors. The owners offer advice on day trips out, and how to get the best bargains which can be had on the railway.

Special offers
Rates per night for a dog are the same in low, mid and high season – currently 2 euros per night.

You might like to know
One of the best ways to discover the spectacular sights of the Jungfrau region is on the Jungfrau mountain railway!

☑ **Dogs welcome** *(subject to conditions)*
☑ **Dogs welcome all season**
☐ **Dogs welcome part season**
☐ **Breed restrictions**
　(e.g. only small dogs accepted)
☑ **Number restrictions** *(max. 1 or 2 dogs)*
☐ **Dog sanitary facilities**
　(e.g. waste bins, bags)
☐ **Dog showers**
☐ **On-site dog walking area**
☐ **Kennels**
☐ **Vet nearby**
　(able to help with UK Pet Passports)

Facilities: Two good sanitary blocks are both heated with free hot showers, good facilities for disabled customers and a baby room. Laundry. Campers' kitchen with microwave, cooker, fridge and utensils. Motorcaravan service point. Well stocked shop. TV and games room. Play area. Small swimming pool. Bicycle hire (June-Aug). Free WiFi. Free bus in the Interlaken area – bus stop 5 walking minutes from camping.
Off site: Cycle trails and way-marked footpaths. Riding 500 m. Golf and bicycle hire 1 km. Lake Thun for fishing 1.5 km. Boat launching 1.5 km. Interlaken and leisure centre 2 km.

Open: 1 May - 15 October.

Directions: Site is on north side of Lake Thun. From road 8 (Thun - Interlaken) on south side of lake take exit 24 Interlaken West. Follow towards lake at roundabout then follow signs for campings. Lazy Rancho is Camp 4. The last 500 m. is a little narrow but no problem. GPS: 46.68605, 7.830633

Charges guide

Per unit incl. 2 persons and electricity	CHF 26,50 - 47,70
extra person	CHF 6,00 - 6,60
child (6-15 yrs)	CHF 3,50 - 3,80
dog	CHF 3,00

SWITZERLAND – Brienz am See

Camping Aaregg

Seestrasse 28a, CH-3855 Brienz am See (Bern)
t: 033 951 1843   e: mail@aaregg.ch
alanrogers.com/CH9510   www.aaregg.ch

Accommodation: ☑Pitch ☑Mobile home/chalet ☐ Hotel/B&B ☐ Apartment

Brienz, in the Bernese Oberland, is a delightful little town on the lake of the same name and the centre of the Swiss wood carving industry. Camping Aaregg is an excellent site situated on the southern shores of the lake with splendid views across the water to the mountains. There are 65 static caravans occupying their own area and 180 tourist pitches, all with electricity (10/16A). Of these, 16 are larger with hardstandings, water and drainage, and many of these have good lake views. Pitches fronting the lake have a surcharge. The trees and flowers make an attractive and peaceful environment. An excellent base from which to explore the many attractions of this scenic region, and is a useful night stop when passing from Interlaken to Luzern. Nearby at Ballenberg is the fascinating Freilichtmuseum, a very large open-air park of old Swiss houses which have been brought from all over Switzerland and re-erected in groups. Traditional Swiss crafts are demonstrated in some of these.

You might like to know
This is a friendly, family campsite on the banks of the beautiful Brienzersee, with some great spots for dog walking.

☑ **Dogs welcome** (subject to conditions)
☑ **Dogs welcome all season**
☐ **Dogs welcome part season**
☐ **Breed restrictions**
  (e.g. only small dogs accepted)
☑ **Number restrictions** (max. 1 or 2 dogs)
☑ **Dog sanitary facilities**
  (e.g. waste bins, bags)
☐ **Dog showers**
☐ **On-site dog walking area**
☐ **Kennels**
☐ **Vet nearby**
  (able to help with UK Pet Passports)

Facilities: New, very attractive sanitary facilities built and maintained to first class standards. Showers with washbasins. Washbasins (open style and in cubicles). Children's section. Family shower rooms. Baby changing room. Facilities for disabled visitors. Laundry facilities. Motorcaravan services. Pleasant restaurant with terrace and takeaway in season. Play area. Fishing. Bicycle hire. Boat launching. Lake swimming in clear water (unsupervised). English is spoken.
Off site: Frequent train services to Interlaken and Lucerne as well as boat cruises from Brienz to Interlaken and back. Motorboat hire is possible, and waterskiing on the lake.

Open: 1 April - 31 October.

Directions: Site is on road B6/B11 on the east of Brienz. Entrance is just about opposite the Esso filling station, well signed. From the Interlaken-Luzern motorway, take Brienz exit and turn towards Brienz, site then on the left. GPS: 46.75000, 8.03332

Charges guide

Per unit incl. 2 persons

and electricity	CHF 34,40 - 59,00
per person	CHF 7,70 - 11,00
child (6-16 yrs)	CHF 4,90 - 7,00
dog	CHF 2,80 - 4,00

Camping Eienwäldli

Wasserfallstrasse 108, CH-6390 Engelberg (Unterwalden)
t: **041 637 1949** e: **info@eienwaeldli.ch**
alanrogers.com/CH9570 www.eienwaeldli.ch

Accommodation: ☑Pitch ☑Mobile home/chalet ☐Hotel/B&B ☐Apartment

This super site has facilities which must make it one of the best in Switzerland. It is situated in a beautiful location 3,500 feet above sea level, surrounded by mountains on the edge of the delightful village of Engelberg. Half of the site is taken up by static caravans which are grouped together at one side. The camping area is in two parts – nearest the entrance there are 57 hardstandings for caravans and motorcaravans, all with electricity (metered) and beyond this is a flat meadow for about 70 tents. Reception can be found in the very modern foyer of the Eienwäldli Hotel which also houses the indoor pool, health complex, shop and café/bar. The indoor pool has been most imaginatively rebuilt as a Felsenbad spa bath with adventure pool, steam and relaxing grottoes, Kneipp's cure, children's pool with water slides, solarium, Finnish sauna and eucalyptus steam bath (charged for). Being about 35 km. from Luzern by road and with a rail link, it makes a quiet, peaceful base from which to explore the Vierwaldstattersee region, walk in the mountains or just enjoy the scenery.

You might like to know
A maximum of one dog per pitch is allowed here.

☑ **Dogs welcome** *(subject to conditions)*
☑ **Dogs welcome all season**
☐ **Dogs welcome part season**
☐ **Breed restrictions**
   (e.g. only small dogs accepted)
☐ **Number restrictions** *(max. 1 or 2 dogs)*
☐ **Dog sanitary facilities**
   (e.g. waste bins, bags)
☐ **Dog showers**
☐ **On-site dog walking area**
☐ **Kennels**
☐ **Vet nearby**
   (able to help with UK Pet Passports)

Facilities: The main toilet block, heated in cool weather, is situated at the rear of the hotel and has free hot water in washbasins (in cabins) and (on payment) showers. A new modern toilet block has been added near the top end of the site. Washing machines and dryers. Shop. Café/bar. Small lounge. Indoor pool complex. Ski facilities including a drying room. Large play area with a rafting pool fed by fresh water from the mountain stream. Torches useful. TV. WiFi. Golf. Off site: Golf driving range and 18-hole course near. Fishing and bicycle hire 1 km. Riding 2 km.

Open: All year.

Directions: From N2 Gotthard motorway, leave at exit 33 Stans-Sud and follow signs to Engelberg. Turn right at T-junction on edge of town and follow signs to 'Wasserfall' and site. GPS: 46.80940, 8.42367

Charges guide

Per person	CHF 6,00 - 9,00
child (6-15 yrs)	CHF 3,00 - 4,50
pitch	CHF 10,00 - 17,00
dog	CHF 1,30 - 2,00

Credit cards accepted (surcharge).

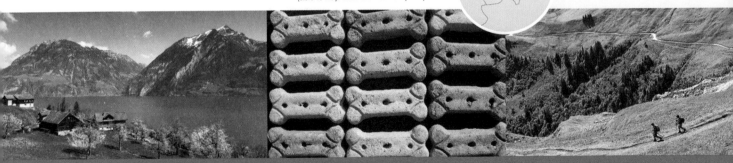

Balatontourist Camping Napfény

Halász u. 5, H-8253 Révfülöp (Veszprem County)
t: 87 563 031 e: napfeny@balatontourist.hu
alanrogers.com/HU5370 www.balatontourist.hu

Accommodation: ☑Pitch ☑Mobile home/chalet ☐ Hotel/B&B ☐ Apartment

Camping Napfény, an exceptionally good site, is designed for families with children of all ages looking for an active holiday, and has a 200 m. frontage on Lake Balaton. The site's 395 pitches vary in size (60-110 m²) and almost all have shade – very welcome during the hot Hungarian summers – and 6-10A electricity. As with most of the sites on Lake Balaton, a train line runs just outside the site boundary. There are steps to get into the lake and canoes, boats and pedaloes for hire. An extensive entertainment programme is designed for all ages and there are several bars and restaurants of various styles. There are souvenir shops and a supermarket. In fact, you need not leave the site at all during your holiday, although there are several excursions on offer, including to Budapest or to one of the many Hungarian spas, a trip over Lake Balaton or a wine tour.

You might like to know

Lake Balaton provides great opportunities for you to take your dog for a walk.

☑ **Dogs welcome** *(subject to conditions)*
☑ **Dogs welcome all season**
☐ **Dogs welcome part season**
☑ **Breed restrictions**
  (e.g. only small dogs accepted)
☑ **Number restrictions** *(max. 1 or 2 dogs)*
☑ **Dog sanitary facilities**
  (e.g. waste bins, bags)
☑ **Dog showers**
☐ **On-site dog walking area**
☐ **Kennels**
☐ **Vet nearby**
  (able to help with UK Pet Passports)

Facilities: The three excellent sanitary blocks have toilets, washbasins (open style and in cabins) with hot and cold water, spacious showers (both preset and controllable), child size toilets and basins, and two bathrooms (hourly charge). Heated baby room. Facilities for disabled campers. Launderette. Dog shower. Motorcaravan services. Supermarket. Several bars, restaurants and souvenir shops. Sports field. Tennis. Minigolf. Fishing. Bicycle hire. Canoe, rowing boats and pedalo hire. Extensive entertainment programme for all ages. Free internet access. Off site: Riding 3 km.

Open: 30 April - 30 September.

Directions: Follow road 71 from Veszprém southeast to Keszthely. Site is in Révfülöp. GPS: 46.82417, 17.63733

Charges guide

Per unit incl. 2 persons and electricity	HUF 3400 - 7150
extra person	HUF 800 - 1200
child (2-14 yrs)	HUF 550 - 900
dog	HUF 550 - 900

Ferienanlage Tiroler Zugspitze

Obermoos 1, A-6632 Ehrwald (Tirol)
t: 056 732 309 e: camping@zugspitze.at
alanrogers.com/AU0040 www.ferienanlage-zugspitze.at

Accommodation: ☑Pitch ☑Mobile home/chalet ☐Hotel/B&B ☐Apartment

Although Ehrwald is in Austria, it is from the entrance of Zugspitzcamping that the cable car runs to the summit of Germany's highest mountain. Standing at 1,200 feet above sea level at the foot of the mountain, the 200 pitches (120 for tourists), mainly of grass over stones, are on flat terraces with fine panoramic views in parts. All have electricity connections (16A). The modern reception building at the entrance also houses a fine restaurant with a terrace which is open to those using the cable car, as well as those staying on the site. A further large modern building, heated in cool weather, has an indoor pool and fitness centre. This excellent mountain site, with its superb facilities, provides a good base from which to explore this interesting part of Austria and Bavaria by car or on foot. A trip up to the Zugspitze offers beautiful views and many opportunities for mountain walking.

You might like to know
There are forest walks and mountain hiking in the immediate area that are ideal for exercising dogs.

- ☑ **Dogs welcome** (subject to conditions)
- ☑ **Dogs welcome all season**
- ☐ **Dogs welcome part season**
- ☐ **Breed restrictions**
  (e.g. only small dogs accepted)
- ☑ **Number restrictions** (max. 1 or 2 dogs)
- ☐ **Dog sanitary facilities**
  (e.g. waste bins, bags)
- ☐ **Dog showers**
- ☐ **On-site dog walking area**
- ☐ **Kennels**
- ☐ **Vet nearby**
  (able to help with UK Pet Passports)

Facilities: Two good sanitary blocks (cleaning may be variable) provide some washbasins in cabins and 20 private bathrooms for rent. Separate children's unit. Baby room. Unit for disabled visitors. Laundry facilities. Drying rooms. Motorcaravan service point. Shop. Bar. Restaurant. Indoor pool with sauna, whirlpool and fitness centre with solarium and massage room. Outdoor pool and children's pool with slide. Internet access. Bicycle hire. Play area. Organised activities in season. Off site: Hotel, souvenir shop and cable car station 100 m. Sports in Ehrwald 5 km.

Open: All year.

Directions: Follow signs in Ehrwald to Tiroler Zugspitzbahn and then signs to site.
GPS: 47.42521, 10.93809

Charges guide

Per person	€ 10,00 - € 12,00
child (4-15 yrs)	€ 7,50 - € 8,50
pitch	€ 6,00 - € 8,00
electricity per kWh	€ 0,80
dog	€ 4,00

Special seasonal weekly offers.
Mastercard accepted.

AUSTRIA – Natters

Ferienparadies Natterer See

Natterer See 1, A-6161 Natters (Tirol)
t: 051 254 6732 e: info@natterersee.com
alanrogers.com/AU0060 www.natterersee.com

Accommodation: ☑Pitch ☑Mobile home/chalet ☐ Hotel/B&B ☐ Apartment

Above Innsbruck, 7 km. southwest of the town, this excellent site is in a quiet and isolated location around two small lakes. Founded in 1930, the site is renowned as one of Austria's finest campsites and in 2007 the owners embarked on an ambitious improvement project with 40 new, large 'super' pitches. Each with a minimum size of 110 m², these pitches are equipped with water, drainage, electricity and cable TV connection. There are a further 235 individual pitches of varying sizes, either on flat ground by the lake or on higher, level terraces. The standard pitches have 6A electricity. Many are reinforced by gravel. There are many fine mountain views and a wide variety of scenic excursions. For the more active, signed walks start from the site. One of the lakes is used for swimming with a long 67 m. slide (free to campers, on payment to day visitors). For winter camping the site offers ski and drying rooms and a free ski-bus service. A toboggan run and langlauf have been developed with ice skating, ice hockey and curling on the lake. Very good English is spoken.

You might like to know
Woodland, mountains and alpine pastures are all in the immediate area and are suitable for dog walking. Dogs are allowed in caravan accomodation all year round.

☑ **Dogs welcome** *(subject to conditions)*
☑ **Dogs welcome all season**
☐ **Dogs welcome part season**
☐ **Breed restrictions**
    (e.g. only small dogs accepted)
☑ **Number restrictions** *(max. 1 or 2 dogs)*
☐ **Dog sanitary facilities**
    (e.g. waste bins, bags)
☐ **Dog showers**
☐ **On-site dog walking area**
☐ **Kennels**
☐ **Vet nearby**
    (able to help with UK Pet Passports)

Facilities: The large sanitary blocks have underfloor heating, some washbasins in cabins, plus excellent facilities for babies, children and disabled campers. Laundry facilities. Motorcaravan services. Bar. Restaurant and takeaway (20/3-3/10). Pizzeria. Good shop. Archery. Youth room with games, pool and billiards. TV room with Sky. Internet point and WiFi. Open air cinema. Mountain bike hire. 'Aquapark' (1/5-30/9). Surf bikes and wind-glider. Canoes and mini sailboats for rent. Dogs are not accepted in high season (July/Aug).
Off site: Riding 6 km. Golf 12 km. Bus to Innsbruck.

Open: All year excl. 1 November - 14 December.

Directions: From Inntal autobahn (A12) take Brenner autobahn (A13) as far as Innsbruck-sud/Natters exit (no. 3) without payment. Turn left by Shell petrol station onto the B182 to Natters. At roundabout take first exit and immediately right again and follow signs to site 4 km.
GPS: 47.23755, 11.34201

Charges guide

Per unit incl. 2 persons and electricity	€ 25,20 - € 42,00
extra person	€ 5,90 - € 8,20
child (under 13 yrs)	€ 4,60 - € 6,00
dog (excl. July/Aug)	€ 3,50 - € 4,00

AUSTRIA – Prutz

Aktiv-Camping Prutz

Pontlatzstrasse 22, A-6522 Prutz (Tirol)
t: 054 722 648 e: info@aktiv-camping.at
alanrogers.com/AU0155 www.aktiv-camping.at

Accommodation: ☑Pitch ☑Mobile home/chalet ☐Hotel/B&B ☐Apartment

Aktiv-Camping is a long site which lies beside, and is fenced off from, the River Inn. Most of the 100 individual level pitches are for touring and range in size from 80-100 m². They all have 6A electrical connections and in the larger area fit together sideways and back to back. As a result, the site can sometimes have the appearance of being quite crowded. There is a separate overnight area for motorcaravans. This is an attractive area with many activities in both summer and winter for all age groups. You may well consider using this site not just as an overnight stop, but also for a longer stay. From Roman times onwards, when the Via Augusta passed through, this border region's stategic importance has left behind many fortifications that today feature among its many tourist attractions. Others include walking, cycling and mountain biking, swimming in lakes and pools, as well interesting, educational and adventurous activities for children. The Tiroler Summer card is available without charge at reception giving free offers and discounts for many attractions.

You might like to know
The campsite is open all year long, good for a winter holiday too.

☑ **Dogs welcome** *(subject to conditions)*
☑ **Dogs welcome all season**
☐ **Dogs welcome part season**
☐ **Breed restrictions**
   (e.g. only small dogs accepted)
☑ **Number restrictions** *(max. 1 or 2 dogs)*
☐ **Dog sanitary facilities**
   (e.g. waste bins, bags)
☑ **Dog showers**
☐ **On-site dog walking area**
☐ **Kennels**
☐ **Vet nearby**
   (able to help with UK Pet Passports)

Facilities: The sanitary facilities are of a high standard, with private cabins and good facilities for disabled visitors. Baby room. Washing machine. Dog shower. Small shop. Bar. Takeaway. Play room. Ski room. Skating rink. Internet point. Children's entertainment. Guided walks, skiing (free shuttle service). WiFi. Off site: Indoor pool at Feichten, Pilgrim's Church at Kaltenbrunn. Kaunertaler Glacier.

Open: All year.

Directions: Travelling west from Innsbruck on the E60/A12 for about 65 km. turn south onto the B180 signed Bregenz, Arlberg, Innsbruck and Fernpass for 11 km. to Prutz. Site is signed from the B180 over the bridge.
GPS: 47.08833, 10.65831

Charges guide

Per unit incl. 2 persons and electricity	€ 15,50 - € 25,10
extra person	€ 3,90 - € 6,90
child (5-14 yrs)	€ 2,50 - € 3,50
dog	€ 2,00 - € 3,00

AUSTRIA – Bruck

Sportcamp Woferlgut

Kroessenbach 40, A-5671 Bruck (Salzburg)
t: 065 457 3030 e: info@sportcamp.at
alanrogers.com/AU0180 www.sportcamp.at

Accommodation: ☑Pitch ☑Mobile home/chalet ☐ Hotel/B&B ☐ Apartment

The village of Bruck lies at the junction of the B311 and the Grossglocknerstrasse in the Hohe Tauern National Park. Sportcamp Woferlgut, a family run site, is one of the best in Austria. Although surrounded by mountains, the site is quite flat with pleasant views. The 350 level, grass pitches are marked out by shrubs (300 for touring units) and each has electricity (16A), water, drainage, cable TV socket and gas point. A high grass bank separates the site and the road. The site's own lake, used for swimming and fishing, is surrounded by a landscaped sunbathing area. The fitness centre has a fully equipped gym, whilst another building contains a sauna and cold dip, Turkish bath, solarium (all free) massage on payment and a bar. In summer there is a free activity programme, evenings with live music, club for children, weekly barbecues and guided cycle and mountain tours. In winter a cross country skiing trail and toboggan run lead from the site and a free bus service is provided to nearby skiing facilities. With Salzburg to the north and Innsbruck to the northwest, this a splendid base for a family holiday.

You might like to know
The site is surrounded by alpine pastures and wooded areas ideal for dog walking. The National Park is nearby and is excellent for hiking.

☑ **Dogs welcome** *(subject to conditions)*
☑ **Dogs welcome all season**
☐ **Dogs welcome part season**
☐ **Breed restrictions**
    (e.g. only small dogs accepted)
☑ **Number restrictions** *(max. 1 or 2 dogs)*
☐ **Dog sanitary facilities**
    (e.g. waste bins, bags)
☐ **Dog showers**
☐ **On-site dog walking area**
☐ **Kennels**
☐ **Vet nearby**
    (able to help with UK Pet Passports)

Facilities: Three modern sanitary blocks (the newest in a class of its own) have excellent facilities, including private cabins, underfloor heating and music. Washing machines and dryers. Facilities for disabled visitors. Family bathrooms for hire. Motorcaravan services. Well stocked shop. Bar, restaurant and takeaway. Small, heated outdoor pool and children's pool (28/4-30/9). Fitness centre. Two playgrounds, indoor play room and children's cinema. Tennis. Bicycle hire. Fishing. Watersports and lake swimming. Collection of small animals with pony rides for young children. Off site: ATM 500 m. Skiing 2.5 km. Golf 3 km. Boat launching and sailing 3.5 km. Hiking and skiing (all year) nearby.

Open: All year.

Directions: Site is southwest of Bruck. From road B311, Bruck by-pass, take southern exit (Grossglockner) and site is signed from the junction of B311 and B107 roads (small signs). GPS: 47.2838, 12.81694

Charges guide

Per unit incl. 2 persons and electricity (plus meter)	€ 21,90 - € 34,50
extra person	€ 5,10 - € 8,20
child (2-10 yrs)	€ 4,10 - € 6,10
dog	€ 3,10 - € 4,30

FRANCE – Vence

Camping Domaine de la Bergerie

1330 chemin de la Sine, F-06140 Vence (Alpes-Maritimes)
t: 04 93 58 09 36 e: info@camping-domainedelabergerie.com
alanrogers.com/FR06030 www.camping-domainedelabergerie.com

Accommodation: ☑Pitch ☑Mobile home/chalet ☐Hotel/B&B ☐Apartment

La Bergerie is a quiet, family owned site, situated in the hills 3 km. from Vence and 10 km. from the sea at Cagnes-sur-Mer. With no mobile homes or chalets, this extensive, natural, lightly wooded site is in a secluded position about 300 m. above sea level. Most of the pitches are shaded and all are of a good size. There are 450 pitches, 224 with electricity (2/5A), water and drainage. Because of the nature of this site, some pitches are a little distance from the toilet blocks. With the aim of keeping this a quiet and tranquil place to stay, there are no organised activities and definitely no groups allowed. It is a large site but because it is so extensive it does not give that impression. An hourly bus service (excluding Sundays) runs from the site to Vence.

Special offers
10% discount in low season for stays over 10 nights. 20% discount from 25 March-30 April and from 1-15 October.

You might like to know
Dogs are allowed at the Lac d'Allos (but not elsewhere in the Parc du Mercantour) and on some beaches. No charge is made for dogs but they must be on a lead on site.

☑ **Dogs welcome** (subject to conditions)
☑ **Dogs welcome all season**
☐ **Dogs welcome part season**
☑ **Breed restrictions**
   (e.g. only small dogs accepted)
☑ **Number restrictions** (max. 1 or 2 dogs)
☐ **Dog sanitary facilities**
   (e.g. waste bins, bags)
☐ **Dog showers**
☑ **On-site dog walking area**
☐ **Kennels**
☑ **Vet nearby**
   (able to help with UK Pet Passports)

Facilities: Refurbished toilet blocks, excellent provision for disabled campers (pitches near the block can be reserved). Good shop. Small bar/restaurant, takeaway (all 1/5-30/9). Large swimming pool, paddling pool, spacious sunbathing area (1/5-30/9). Playground. Bicycle hire. Tennis. 12 shaded boules pitches (lit at night) with competitions in season. Barbecues are not permitted. Off site: Riding and fishing 10 km. Golf 18 km.

Open: 25 March - 15 October.

Directions: From A8 exit 47 take Cagnes-sur-Mer road towards Vence. Site is west of Vence. Follow 'toutes directions' around the town, join D2210 Grasse road. In 2 km. at roundabout, turn left, follow site signs, 1.5 km. Site on right in light woodland. GPS: 43.71174, 7.0905

Charges guide

Per unit incl. 2 persons and electricity	€ 19,00 - € 26,00

Less 10-15% for longer stays.

54

Camping Ascou la Forge

F-09110 Ascou (Ariège)
t: 05 61 64 60 03   e: info@ascou-la-forge.fr
alanrogers.com/FR09120   www.ascou-la-forge.fr

Accommodation: ☑Pitch ☑Mobile home/chalet ☐ Hotel/B&B ☐ Apartment

The site sits in a delightful, tranquil valley among the foothills of the Pyrénées and is just east of the interesting village of La Bastide-de-Sérou, beside the River Arize (good trout fishing). The river is fenced for the safety of children on the site, but may be accessed just outside the gate. The 70 large pitches are neatly laid out on level grass within the spacious site. All have 3/6A electricity and are separated into bays by hedges and young trees. An extension to the site gives 24 large, fully serviced pitches (10A) and a small toilet block. You will receive a warm welcome from Dominique and Brigitte at this friendly little family site and Brigitte speaks excellent English. Discounts have been negotiated for several of the local attractions (details are provided in the comprehensive pack provided on arrival – in your own language). This is a comfortable and relaxing base for touring this beautiful part of the Pyrénées with easy access to the medieval town of Foix and even Andorra for duty-free shopping. Deer and wild boar are common in this area and may be sighted in quieter periods.

Special offers
Dogs stay for free in low season. Dog walks are organised.

You might like to know
Dogs are allowed on site and in rental accommodation. Dogs can take a refreshing swim in the river and the reservoir. Many mountain lakes and rivers. More than two dogs require permission.

☑ **Dogs welcome** *(subject to conditions)*
☑ **Dogs welcome all season**
☐ **Dogs welcome part season**
☐ **Breed restrictions**
   (e.g. only small dogs accepted)
☑ **Number restrictions** *(max. 1 or 2 dogs)*
☐ **Dog sanitary facilities**
   (e.g. waste bins, bags)
☐ **Dog showers**
☑ **On-site dog walking area**
☐ **Kennels**
☑ **Vet nearby**
   (able to help with UK Pet Passports)

Facilities: Modern, bright, sanitary block is fully equipped including facilities for disabled visitors which double as a family shower room with a baby bath. Shop. Bar with large screen for major sports events and films about the local flora/fauna. Play area. Maps and walking routes are available from reception. Free WiFi. Off site: Restaurant next door to site (all year). Restaurants, bars and shops in Ax-les-Thermes 7 km.

Open: All year.

Directions: From Ax-Les-Thermes take the D613 signed Quérigat, Quillan and Ascou-Pailhéres. After 3.6 km. turn right on D25 to site on right after 3.4 km. GPS: 42.72444, 1.89274

Charges guide

Per unit incl. 2 persons and electricity	€ 15,00 - € 23,00
extra person	€ 3,50 - € 5,00
child (0-7 yrs)	€ 2,50 - € 3,50
dog	€ 1,00 - € 1,50

FRANCE – Royan-Pontaillac

Camping Clairefontaine

6 rue du Colonel Lachaud, F-17200 Royan-Pontaillac (Charente-Maritime)
t: 05 46 39 08 11   e: info@camping-clairefontaine.com
alanrogers.com/FR17100   www.camping-clairefontaine.com

Accommodation: ☑Pitch ☑Mobile home/chalet ☐ Hotel/B&B ☐ Apartment

Camping Clairefontaine is situated on the outskirts of Royan, 300 m. from a golden sandy beach and casino. Although it is a busy area, the site is peaceful and relaxing. There are 300 pitches, of which 282 are available for touring. Electricity is available to all pitches, but some may require long leads. The site is mostly shaded and level with easy access to pitches. American motorhomes are accepted but care is needed on the entrance road to the site as it is not wide enough for two vehicles to pass. The reception area is large and welcoming and English is spoken. A programme of entertainment is provided in July and August and includes karaoke, singers and folk groups. There are many places of interest to visit, notably the nature reserves, the lighthouse at Cordouan, forests and the oyster beds of Marennes and Oléron.

You might like to know
Please note a maximum of 1 dog per pitch (or mobile home) is allowed. Dogs must be kept on a lead on site.

☑ **Dogs welcome** (subject to conditions)

☑ **Dogs welcome all season**

☐ **Dogs welcome part season**

☑ **Breed restrictions**
   (e.g. only small dogs accepted)

☑ **Number restrictions** (max. 1 or 2 dogs)

☐ **Dog sanitary facilities**
   (e.g. waste bins, bags)

☐ **Dog showers**

☐ **On-site dog walking area**

☐ **Kennels**

☐ **Vet nearby**
   (able to help with UK Pet Passports)

Facilities: Two modern sanitary blocks. Good facilities for disabled visitors. Washing machines. Ironing room. Motorcaravan services. Shop. Bar. Restaurant with takeaway. Swimming and paddling pools. Four play areas. Tennis. Basketball. Entertainment in high season. Internet access. Off site: Beach and sailing 300 m. Bicycle hire 350 m. Fishing 2 km. Riding and golf 10 km.

Open: 24 May - 12 September.

Directions: Exit Royan on Avenue de Pontaillac towards La Palmyre. Turn right at the casino on the front, up Avenue Louise. Site is on left after 200 m. and is signed.
GPS: 45.631388, -1.050122

Charges guide

Per unit incl. 2 persons and electricity	€ 32,00 - € 35,00
extra person	€ 9,00 - € 9,50
child (2-10 yrs)	€ 5,00 - € 5,50
dog	€ 3,00

Camping Port-Punay

Allée Bernard Moreau, les Boucholeurs, F-17340 Châtelaillon-Plage (Charente-Maritime)
t: 05 46 56 01 53   e: contact@camping-port-punay.com
alanrogers.com/FR17340   www.camping-port-punay.com

Accommodation: ☑Pitch ☑Mobile home/chalet ☐ Hotel/B&B ☐ Apartment

Port-Punay is a friendly, well run site just 200 metres from the beach and 3 km. from the centre of the resort of Chatelaillon-Plage. There are 166 touring pitches laid out on well trimmed grass, with many mature poplars and low shrubs. The site has a well stocked shop, open all season, and a small bar and restaurant only open in high season. A heated swimming pool has a separate gated area for paddling. There is a good range of activities available and in high season some entertainment is arranged. This is a family run site (Famille Moreau) and the son of the family speaks excellent English, as does his Dutch wife. Rochefort to the south and La Rochelle to the north are well worth a visit (buses from outside the site), as is the nearby town of Châtelaillon-Plage, which has an all-year covered market and, in summer, a street market every day. Port-Punay has just one large toilet block, centrally positioned on the site, with very good facilities.

You might like to know

This site has a great location with many great places to visit - maybe the Marais Poitevein or green Venice or the fine city of La Rochelle. Dogs are not permitted in mobile homes.

☑ **Dogs welcome** *(subject to conditions)*
☑ **Dogs welcome all season**
☐ **Dogs welcome part season**
☑ **Breed restrictions**
(e.g. only small dogs accepted)
☑ **Number restrictions** *(max. 1 or 2 dogs)*
☐ **Dog sanitary facilities**
(e.g. waste bins, bags)
☐ **Dog showers**
☐ **On-site dog walking area**
☐ **Kennels**
☐ **Vet nearby**
(able to help with UK Pet Passports)

Facilities: One large toilet block with good facilities including washbasins in cubicles and large shower cubicles. Facilities for disabled visitors and babies. Washing machines. Shop. Bar, restaurant and takeaway (15/6-15/9). Swimming pool (heated May-Sept). Games area. Play area. Bicycle hire. Internet access. WiFi. Off site: Beach 200 m. Châtelaillon-Plage 3 km. by road, 1.5 km. along the seafront on foot or bike. Buses to Rochefort and La Rochelle from outside site. Riding 2 km. Golf 10 km.

Open: 1 April - 28 September.

Directions: From N137 (La Rochelle - Rochefort) take exit for Châtelaillon-Plage. At the first roundabout follow the sign for the town centre. At the 2nd roundabout turn left. Follow signs to the site at the seaside hamlet of Les Boucholeurs. Here drive to the sea-wall then turn left through village to site. Take care, as the road has many traffic-calming measures and can be narrow in places. GPS: 46.05480, -1.08340

Charges guide

Per unit incl. 2 persons	€ 14,90 - € 22,00
extra person	€ 4,20 - € 5,50
child (0-3 yrs)	€ 3,20 - € 4,20
electricity (10A)	€ 4,00 - € 5,00

Chadotel le Domaine d'Oléron

La Jousselinière, F-17190 Saint Georges-d'Oléron (Charente-Maritime)
t: 05 46 76 54 97   e: contact@chadotel.com
alanrogers.com/FR17470   www.chadotel.com

Accommodation: ☑Pitch ☑Mobile home/chalet ☐ Hotel/B&B ☐ Apartment

This is a neat, well presented and well managed site where you will receive a warm and friendly welcome from Anneke and Freddy. It is set in a peaceful rural location between Saint Pierre and Saint Georges and is part of the Chadotel group. At present there are 70 pitches of which 40 are for touring. There are plans to include further touring pitches but at present the site appears quite spacious with facilities being under used. Pitches are generously sized (100-150 m²) and are mostly shaded. Level and easily accessible, all have 10A electricity. The site is surrounded by the Forest of Saumonards and is just 3 km. from the beach. The local port, shops and restaurants are also nearby. Boat trips are available around the island to see Fort Boyard, Chasson Lighthouse and the Château d'Oléron.

You might like to know

Why not take a boat trip around Fort Boyard or visit the salt marshes, oyster farms and fishing ports?

☑ **Dogs welcome** (subject to conditions)
☑ **Dogs welcome all season**
☐ **Dogs welcome part season**
☑ **Breed restrictions**
  (e.g. only small dogs accepted)
☑ **Number restrictions** (max. 1 or 2 dogs)
☐ **Dog sanitary facilities**
  (e.g. waste bins, bags)
☐ **Dog showers**
☐ **On-site dog walking area**
☐ **Kennels**
☐ **Vet nearby**
  (able to help with UK Pet Passports)

Facilities: Modern sanitary block with facilities for disabled visitors and babies. Washing machines. Ironing room. Snack bar. Bar with TV. Takeaway. Bread delivered daily. Swimming pool with slides. Adventure style play area. Six petanque lanes. Bicycle hire. Organised entertainment two or three times a week in July/Aug. Gas barbecues only on pitches, communal areas for charcoal. Off site: Royan Zoo. Fishing and riding 2 km. Cycle trails. Golf 8 km.

Open: 3 April - 25 September.

Directions: Take D734 to St Pierre. Turn right in St Pierre after Le Clerc supermarket. At next roundabout turn left towards Le Bois Fleury. After passing airfield, turn right and left and site is on the left. GPS: 45.9674685, -1.3192605

Charges guide

Per unit incl. 2 persons and electricity	€ 15,80 - € 29,90
extra person	€ 5,80
child (2-13 yrs)	€ 3,80
dog	€ 3,00

Camping Antioche d'Oléron

Route de Proires, F-17840 La Brée-les-Bains (Charente-Maritime)
t: **05 46 47 92 00** e: **info@camping-antiochedoleron.com**
alanrogers.com/FR17570 www.camping-antiochedoleron.com

Accommodation: ☑Pitch ☑Mobile home/chalet ☐ Hotel/B&B ☐ Apartment

Situated to the northeast of the island, Camping Antioche is quietly located within a five minute walk to the beach. There are 130 pitches, of which 73 are occupied by mobile homes and 57 are for touring units. The pitches are set amongst attractive shrubs and palm trees and all have electricity (10A), water and a drain. A new pool area which comprises two swimming pools (heated), two jacuzzis, two paddling pools and a raised sunbathing deck, is beautifully landscaped with palms and flowers. A small bar, restaurant and takeaway offer reasonably priced food and drinks. The site becomes livelier in season with regular evening entertainment and activities for all the family. With specially prepared trails for cycling, oyster farms and salt flats to visit, the Ile d'Oléron offers something for everyone. Bresnais market, selling local produce and products, is within easy access on foot and is held daily in high season.

You might like to know
Dogs are welcome but a vaccination certificate is required and they must be kept on a lead on site.

☑ **Dogs welcome** *(subject to conditions)*
☑ **Dogs welcome all season**
☐ **Dogs welcome part season**
☑ **Breed restrictions**
   (e.g. only small dogs accepted)
☑ **Number restrictions** *(max. 1 or 2 dogs)*
☐ **Dog sanitary facilities**
   (e.g. waste bins, bags)
☐ **Dog showers**
☐ **On-site dog walking area**
☐ **Kennels**
☐ **Vet nearby**
   (able to help with UK Pet Passports)

Facilities: The single sanitary block is of a good standard and is kept clean and fresh. Facilities for disabled visitors. Laundry. Motorcaravan services. Bar, restaurant and snack bar (weekends only May and June, daily July/Aug). Swimming and paddling pools. Games room. Play area. WiFi. Bicycle hire (July/Aug). Off site: Beach 150 m. Fishing 150 m. Riding 1.5 km.Golf 7 km.

Open: 1 April - 30 September.

Directions: Cross the bridge on the D26 and join the D734. After St Georges turn right onto the D273E1 towards La Bree-les-Baines. At T-junction turn left from where the campsite is signed. GPS: 46.02007, -1.35764

Charges guide

Per unit incl. 2 persons and electricity	€ 21,15 - € 35,15
extra person	€ 7,10
child (1-14 yrs)	€ 3,70
dog	€ 4,00

FRANCE – Saint Pardoux

Kawan Village Chateau le Verdoyer

Champs Romain, F-24470 Saint Pardoux (Dordogne)
t: 05 53 56 94 64 e: chateau@verdoyer.fr
alanrogers.com/FR24010 www.verdoyer.fr

Accommodation: ☑Pitch ☑Mobile home/chalet ☑Hotel/B&B ☐ Apartment

The twenty six-hectare estate has three lakes, two for fishing and one with a sandy beach and safe swimming area. There are 135 good sized touring pitches, level, terraced and hedged. With a choice of wooded area or open field, all have electricity (5/10A) and most share a water supply between four pitches. There is a swimming pool complex and in high season activities are organised for children (5-13 yrs) but there is no disco. This site is well adapted for those with disabilities, with two fully adapted chalets, wheelchair access to all facilities and even a lift into the pool. Le Verdoyer has been developed in the park of a restored château and is owned by a Dutch family. We particularly like this site for its beautiful buildings and lovely surroundings. It is situated in the lesser known area of the Dordogne sometimes referred to as the Périgord Vert, with its green forests and small lakes. The courtyard area between reception and the bar houses evening activities, and is a pleasant place to enjoy drinks and relax. The château itself has rooms to let and its excellent lakeside restaurant is also open to the public.

Facilities: Well appointed toilet blocks include facilities for disabled visitors, and baby baths. Serviced launderette. Motorcaravan services. Fridge rental. Shop with gas (1/5-30/9). Bar, snacks, takeaway and restaurant (1/5-30/9). Bistro (July/Aug). Two pools the smaller covered in low season, slide, paddling pool. Play areas. Tennis. Minigolf. Bicycle hire. Small library. WiFi (charged), Computer in reception for internet access. International newspapers daily. Off site: Riding 5 km. 'Circuit des Orchidées' (22 species of orchid). Market (Thur and Sun) at Saint Pardoux 12 km.

Open: 23 April - 6 October.

Directions: Site is 2 km. from the Limoges (N21) - Chalus (D6bis-D85) - Nontron road, 20 km. south of Chalus and is well signed from main road. Site on the D96 about 4 km. north of village of Champs Romain. GPS: 45.55035, 0.7947

Charges guide

Per unit incl. 2 persons and electricity	€ 21,00 - € 32,00
extra person	€ 5,00 - € 6,50
child (6-11 yrs)	€ 4,00 - € 5,00
dog	free - € 4,00

Special offers
One dog free of charge in low season.

You might like to know
Many excellent walks lead directly from the campsite.

☑ **Dogs welcome** *(subject to conditions)*
☑ **Dogs welcome all season**
☐ **Dogs welcome part season**
☐ **Breed restrictions**
  (e.g. only small dogs accepted)
☑ **Number restrictions** *(max. 1 or 2 dogs)*
☑ **Dog sanitary facilities**
  (e.g. waste bins, bags)
☐ **Dog showers**
☑ **On-site dog walking area**
☐ **Kennels**
☑ **Vet nearby**
  (able to help with UK Pet Passports)

Huttopia Senonches

Etang de Badouleau, avenue de Badouleau, F-28250 Senonches (Eure-et-Loir)
t: 04 37 64 22 35 e: senonches@huttopia.com
alanrogers.com/FR28140 www.huttopia.com

Accommodation: ☑Pitch ☑Mobile home/chalet ☐Hotel/B&B ☐Apartment

Senonches is the latest addition to the Huttopia group and first opened for the 2010 season. This site is hidden away in the huge Forêt Dominiale de Senonches and, in keeping with other Huttopia sites, combines a high standard of comfort with a real sense of backwoods camping. There are 126 pitches here, some with electrical connections (6/10A). The pitches are very large ranging from 100 m². to no less than 300 m². There are also ten Canadian style log cabins and tents available for rent. A good range of on-site amenities includes a shop and a bar/restaurant. The pool overlooks a lake and is open from early July until September. The forest can be explored on foot or by cycle (rental available on site) and beyond the forest, the great city of Chartres is easily visited, with its stunning Gothic cathedral, widely considered to be the finest in France.

You might like to know

Senonches is located at the heart of a vast forest with an extensive network of footpaths. One pet is accepted in the rental accommodation.

- ☑ **Dogs welcome** *(subject to conditions)*
- ☑ **Dogs welcome all season**
- ☐ **Dogs welcome part season**
- ☐ **Breed restrictions**
  (e.g. only small dogs accepted)
- ☑ **Number restrictions** *(max. 1 or 2 dogs)*
- ☐ **Dog sanitary facilities**
  (e.g. waste bins, bags)
- ☐ **Dog showers**
- ☐ **On-site dog walking area**
- ☐ **Kennels**
- ☐ **Vet nearby**
  (able to help with UK Pet Passports)

Facilities: The toilet blocks are modern and are heated in low season, with special facilities for disabled visitors. Shop. Bar. Snack bar. Takeaway. Swimming pool. Fishing. Play area. Bicycle hire. Entertainment and activity programme. Tents and chalets for rent. Only one dog is accepted. Off site: Riding 4 km. Senonches (good selection of shops, bars and restaurants). Cycle and walking tracks. Chartres.

Open: 24 April - 5 November.

Directions: Approaching from Chartres, use the ringroad (N154) and then take the D24 in a northwesterly direction. Drive through Digny and continue to Senonches, from where the site is well signed. GPS: 48.5533, 1.04146

Charges guide

Per unit incl. 2 persons	
and electricity	€ 18,00 - € 34,00
extra person	€ 4,00 - € 5,50
child (2-7 yrs)	€ 2,50 - € 3,60

Camping le Moulin

Lieu-dit le Moulin, F-31220 Martres-Tolosane (Haute-Garonne)
t: **05 61 98 86 40** e: **info@campinglemoulin.com**
alanrogers.com/FR31000 www.campinglemoulin.com

Accommodation: ☑Pitch ☑Mobile home/chalet ☐ Hotel/B&B ☐ Apartment

With attractive shaded pitches and many activities, this family-run campsite has 12 hectares of woods and fields beside the River Garonne. It is close to Martres-Tolosane, an interesting medieval village. Some of the 60 level and grassy pitches are 'supersize' and all have electricity (6-10A). There are 24 chalets to rent. Summer brings opportunities for guided canoeing, archery and walking. A large sports field is available all season, with tennis, volleyball, basketball, boules and birdwatching on site. Facilities for visitors with disabilities are very good, although the sanitary block is a little dated. Some road noise. Large grounds for dog walking. Le Moulin is on the site of a 17th-century watermill and the buildings have been traditionally restored. The friendly outdoor bar serves snacks and in summer the restaurant serves full meals. The bar has WiFi. The swimming pool is large with an adjoining children's pool. During the high season, an organised activity and entertainment programme is on offer. Sites et Paysages member.

Special offers
Dogs are welcome all season and are free of charge outside July and August.

You might like to know
Dogs must be kept on a lead within the site. There is a large open space adjacent to the site, along the banks of the Garonne (dogs can take a dip!) - ideal for exercising your dog.

☑ **Dogs welcome** *(subject to conditions)*
☑ **Dogs welcome all season**
☐ **Dogs welcome part season**
☐ **Breed restrictions**
   (e.g. only small dogs accepted)
☑ **Number restrictions** *(max. 1 or 2 dogs)*
☑ **Dog sanitary facilities**
   (e.g. waste bins, bags)
☐ **Dog showers**
☑ **On-site dog walking area**
☐ **Kennels**
☑ **Vet nearby**
   (able to help with UK Pet Passports)

Facilities: Large sanitary block with separate ladies' and gents WCs. Communal area with showers and washbasins in cubicles. Separate heated area for disabled visitors with shower, WC and basin. Baby bath. Laundry facilities. Motorcaravan services. Outdoor bar with WiFi. Snack bar and takeaway (1/6-15/9). Daily bakers van (except Monday). Heated swimming and paddling pools (1/6-15/9). Fishing. Tennis. Canoeing. Archery. Walks in the countryside. BMX track. Playground. Games room. Entertainment programme and children's club (high season). Off site: Martres-Tolosane 1.5 km. Walking trails and cycle routes. Riding 4 km. Golf 12 km.

Open: 1 April - 30 September.

Directions: From the A64 motorway (Toulouse-Tarbes) take exit 21 (Boussens) or exit 22 (Martres-Tolosane) and follow signs to Martres-Tolosane. Site is well signed from village. GPS: 43.19048, 1.01788

Charges guide

Per unit incl. 2 persons and electricity	€ 20,00 - € 36,00
extra person	€ 4,50 - € 6,50
child (under 7 yrs)	€ 2,50 - € 3,50
dog	€ 1,50 - € 2,30

Camping les Sablons

Avenue des Muriers, F-34420 Portiragnes-Plage (Hérault)
t: 04 67 90 90 55   e: contact@les-sablons.com
alanrogers.com/FR34400   www.les-sablons.com

Accommodation: ☑Pitch ☑Mobile home/chalet ☐Hotel/B&B ☐Apartment

Les Sablons is an impressive and popular site with lots going on. Most of the facilities are arranged around the entrance with shops, a restaurant, bar and a large pool complex with no less than five slides, three heated pools and a large stage for entertainment. There is also direct access to the white sandy beach at the back of the site close to a small lake. There is good shade on the majority of the site, although some of the newer touring pitches have less shade but are nearer the gate to the beach. On level sandy grass, all have 6A electricity. Of around 800 pitches, around half are taken by a range of mobile homes and chalets (many for hire, some by British tour operators). A wide range of sporting activities, and evening entertainment is arranged with much for children to do. In fact, this is a real holiday venue aiming to keep all the family happy.

You might like to know

Dogs are not allowed on the beach next to the site, but there are other dog friendly beaches in the area.

☑ **Dogs welcome** *(subject to conditions)*
☑ **Dogs welcome all season**
☐ **Dogs welcome part season**
☐ **Breed restrictions**
  (e.g. only small dogs accepted)
☑ **Number restrictions** *(max. 1 or 2 dogs)*
☐ **Dog sanitary facilities**
  (e.g. waste bins, bags)
☐ **Dog showers**
☐ **On-site dog walking area**
☐ **Kennels**
☐ **Vet nearby**
  (able to help with UK Pet Passports)

Facilities: Well equipped, modernised toilet blocks include large showers some with washbasins. Baby baths. Facilities for disabled visitors. Supermarket, bakery and newsagent. Restaurant, bar and takeaway. Swimming pool complex. Entertainment and activity programme with sports, music and cultural activities. Beach club. Tennis. Archery. Play areas. Electronic games. ATM. Internet access. Off site: Riding 200 m. Bicycle hire 100 m.

Open: 1 April - 30 September.

Directions: From A9 exit 35 (Béziers Est) follow signs for Vias and Agde (N112). After large roundabout pass exit to Cers then take exit for Portiragnes (D37). Follow for about 5 km. and pass over Canal du Midi towards Portiragnes-Plage. Site is on left after roundabout. GPS: 43.28003, 3.36396

Charges guide

Per unit incl. 2 persons and electricity	€ 18,00 - € 46,00
extra person	€ 6,00 - € 10,00
child (5-13 yrs)	free - € 8,00
dog	€ 4,00

FRANCE – Loches-en-Touraine

Kawan Village la Citadelle

Avenue Aristide Briand, F-37600 Loches-en-Touraine (Indre-et-Loire)
t: **02 47 59 05 91**   e: **camping@lacitadelle.com**
alanrogers.com/FR37050   www.lacitadelle.com

Accommodation: ☑Pitch ☑Mobile home/chalet ☐ Hotel/B&B ☐ Apartment

A pleasant, well maintained site, one of La Citadelle's best features is that it is within walking distance of Loches, noted for its perfect architecture and its glorious history, yet at the same time the site has a rural atmosphere. The 86 standard touring pitches are all level, of a good size and with 10A electricity. Numerous trees offer varying degrees of shade. The 30 larger, serviced pitches have 16A electricity but little shade. Mobile homes (28 for hire) occupy the other 48 pitches. Loches, with its château and historic dungeons, is a gentle 500 m. walk along the river. A free bus/little train runs from the campsite to the centre of Loches during the summer. An excellent spa centre and the municipal tennis courts are adjacent to the site and many activities are organised during July and August.

You might like to know
There is a pleasant riverside (River Indre) walk from the site which leads to the delightful town centre. Many other excellent walks in the area.

☑ **Dogs welcome** *(subject to conditions)*
☑ **Dogs welcome all season**
☐ **Dogs welcome part season**
☐ **Breed restrictions**
  (e.g. only small dogs accepted)
☑ **Number restrictions** *(max. 1 or 2 dogs)*
☐ **Dog sanitary facilities**
  (e.g. waste bins, bags)
☐ **Dog showers**
☐ **On-site dog walking area**
☐ **Kennels**
☐ **Vet nearby**
  (able to help with UK Pet Passports)

Facilities: Three sanitary blocks provide mainly British style WCs, washbasins (mostly in cabins) and controllable showers. The block at the 'shady' end could be under pressure in high season. Laundry facilities. Motorcaravan service point. Two baby units and provision for disabled visitors (both in need of attention). Heated swimming pool (May-Sept). Paddling pool and play area (adult supervision strongly recommended). Small bar and snack bar (15/6-15/9). Boules, volleyball and games room. Internet access and TV. Off site: Supermarket, station and buses within 1 km. Bicycle hire 50 m. Riding 5 km. Golf and river beach both 10 km. Large market in Loches on Wednesday and Saturday mornings.

Open: 19 March - 10 October.

Directions: Loches is 45 km. southeast of Tours. Site is well signed from most directions. Do not enter town centre. Approach from roundabout by supermarket at southern end of bypass (D943). Site signed towards town centre and is on right in 800 m. GPS: 47.12303, 1.00223

Charges guide

Per unit incl. 2 persons and electricity	€ 19,50 - € 29,00

Kawan Village du Deffay

B.P. 18 Le Deffay, Sainte Reine-de-Bretagne, F-44160 Pontchâteau (Loire-Atlantique)
t: **02 40 88 00 57** e: **campingdudeffay@wanadoo.fr**
alanrogers.com/FR44090 www.camping-le-deffay.com

Accommodation: ☑Pitch ☑Mobile home/chalet ☑Hotel/B&B ☐ Apartment

A family managed site, Château du Deffay is a refreshing departure from the usual formula in that it is not over organised or supervised and has no tour operator units. The 142 good sized, fairly level pitches have pleasant views and are either on open grass, on shallow terraces divided by hedges, or informally arranged in a central, slightly sloping wooded area. Most have electricity. The facilities are located within the old courtyard area of the smaller château that dates from before 1400. A significant attraction of the site is the large, unfenced lake which is well stocked for fishermen and even has free pedaloes for children. The landscape is wonderfully natural and the site blends well with the rural environment of the estate, lake and farmland which surround it. Alpine type chalets overlook the lake and the larger château (built 1880 and which now offers B&B) stands slightly away from the camping area but provides a wonderful backdrop for an evening stroll. The site is close to the Brière Regional Park, the Guérande Peninsula, and La Baule and is just 20 minutes drive from the nearest beach.

Facilities: The main toilet block is well maintained, if a little dated and is well equipped including washbasins in cabins, provision for disabled campers, and a baby bathroom. Laundry facilities. Shop, bar, small restaurant with takeaway (1/5-20/9). Covered and heated swimming pool (at 28 degrees when we visited) and paddling pool (all season). Play area. TV. Animation in season including miniclub. Torches useful. Off site: Golf 7 km. Riding 10 km. Beach 25 km.

Open: 1 May - 30 September.

Directions: Site is signed from D33 Pontchâteau - Herbignac road near Ste Reine. Also signed from the D773 and N165-E60 (exit 13). GPS: 47.44106, -2.15981

Charges guide

Per unit incl. 2 persons and electricity	€ 18,10 - € 27,80
extra person	€ 3,30 - € 5,50
child (2-12 yrs)	€ 2,30 - € 3,80

You might like to know

One dog free of charge per pitch. A charge is made for additional dogs. Vet in nearby Pontchâteau.

☑ **Dogs welcome** (subject to conditions)
☑ **Dogs welcome all season**
☐ **Dogs welcome part season**
☐ **Breed restrictions**
   (e.g. only small dogs accepted)
☑ **Number restrictions** (max. 1 or 2 dogs)
☐ **Dog sanitary facilities**
   (e.g. waste bins, bags)
☐ **Dog showers**
☐ **On-site dog walking area**
☐ **Kennels**
☑ **Vet nearby**
   (able to help with UK Pet Passports)

Campéole le Brabois

Avenue Paul Muller, F-54600 Villers-les-Nancy (Meurthe-et-Moselle)
t: **03 83 27 18 28** e: **brabois@campeole.com**
alanrogers.com/FR54000 www.camping-brabois.com

Accommodation: ☑Pitch ☑Mobile home/chalet ☐ Hotel/B&B ☐ Apartment

This former municipal site is within the Nancy city boundary and 5 km. from the centre. Situated within a forest area, there is shade in most parts and, although the site is on a slight slope, the 185 good-sized, numbered and separated pitches are level. Of these, 160 pitches have electrical connections (5/15A) and 30 also have water and drainage. Being on one of the main routes from Luxembourg to the south of France, Le Brabois makes a good night stop. However, Nancy is a delightful city in the heart of Lorraine and well worth a longer stay. There are many attractions in the area including the interesting 18th century Place Stanislas (pedestrianised) and 11th century city centre. The British manager has a wide range of tourist literature, publishes a monthly English newsletter and is pleased to help plan visits and day trips. Horse racing takes place every two weeks at the Nancy race track next to the campsite, and good wine is produced nearby.

You might like to know
Dogs are welcome on site but must be kept on a lead within the campsite.

☑ **Dogs welcome** *(subject to conditions)*
☑ **Dogs welcome all season**
☐ **Dogs welcome part season**
☑ **Breed restrictions**
   (e.g. only small dogs accepted)
☑ **Number restrictions** *(max. 1 or 2 dogs)*
☐ **Dog sanitary facilities**
   (e.g. waste bins, bags)
☐ **Dog showers**
☐ **On-site dog walking area**
☐ **Kennels**
☐ **Vet nearby**
   (able to help with UK Pet Passports)

Facilities: Six sanitary blocks provide a mix of British and Turkish style WCs and some washbasins in cubicles. Facilities for babies and disabled visitors. Laundry facilities. Motorcaravan service point. Shop. Bread to order. Restaurant with bar and small shop (15/6-31/8). Library. Playground. Off site: Restaurants, shops 1 km. Walking and cycling. Regular buses to Nancy.

Open: 1 April - 15 October.

Directions: From autoroute A33 take exit 2b for Brabois and continue for 500 m. to 'Quick' restaurant on left. Turn left, pass the racetrack to T-junction, turn right and after 400 m. turn right onto site entrance road.
GPS: 48.66440, 6.14330

Charges guide

Per unit incl. 2 persons	
and electricity	€ 13,60 - € 18,70
extra person	€ 4,00 - € 5,60
child (2-6 yrs)	free - € 3,60
dog	€ 2,50 - € 2,60
hiker	€ 6,00 - € 8,10

Credit card minimum € 15.

Camping Indigo Royat

Route de Gravenoire, F-63130 Royat (Puy-de-Dôme)
t: 04 73 35 97 05 e: royat@camping-indigo.com
alanrogers.com/FR63120 www.camping-indigo.com

Accommodation: ☑Pitch ☑Mobile home/chalet ☐ Hotel/B&B ☐ Apartment

This is a spacious and attractive site sitting high on a hillside on the outskirts of Clermont Ferrand, but close to the beautiful Auvergne countryside. It has nearly 200 terraced pitches on part hardstanding. There are 143 available for touring units, all with 6/10A electricity (long leads may be needed). The pitches are informally arranged in groups, with each group widely separated by attractive trees and shrubs. The bar and terrace overlooks the irregularly shaped swimming pool, paddling pool, sunbathing area, tennis courts and play areas. Although very peaceful off season, the site could be busy and lively in July and August. This site would be ideal for those who would like a taste of both the town and the countryside.

You might like to know
This site is well located for exploring the mountainous region of the Massif Central, with its towering volcanoes. Discover the regions history at Parc Vulcania (less than 20 minutes by car).

☑ **Dogs welcome** (subject to conditions)
☑ **Dogs welcome all season**
☐ **Dogs welcome part season**
☐ **Breed restrictions**
    (e.g. only small dogs accepted)
☑ **Number restrictions** (max. 1 or 2 dogs)
☐ **Dog sanitary facilities**
    (e.g. waste bins, bags)
☐ **Dog showers**
☐ **On-site dog walking area**
☐ **Kennels**
☐ **Vet nearby**
    (able to help with UK Pet Passports)

Facilities: Five well appointed toilet blocks, some heated. They have all the usual amenities but it could be a long walk from some pitches. Small shop. Bar, takeaway. Attractive swimming, paddling pools, sunbathing area. Tennis. Boules. Bicycle hire. Two grassy play areas. Organised entertainment in high season. Internet. Only one dog is accepted. Off site: Royat 20 minutes walk but bus available every 30 minutes in the mornings. Clermont Ferrand, Puy-de-Dôme, Parc des Volcans, Vulcania exhibition.

Open: 2 April - 16 October.

Directions: From A75 exit 2 (Clermont Ferrand) follow signs for Bordeaux (D799). At third roundabout exit left signed Bordeaux. Shortly take exit right then turn right, signed Ceyrat. Leaving Ceyrat, at traffic lights take D941C signed Royat and Puy-de-Dôme. At top of hill turn left (D5) site signed. Entrance 800 m. GPS: 45.7587, 3.05509

Charges guide

Per unit incl. 2 persons and electricity	€ 20,35 - € 26,85
extra person	€ 4,60 - € 5,50
child (2-7 yrs)	€ 2,70 - € 3,60
dog	€ 3,00 - € 4,00

Images credit: R. Ettienne

Camping les Tamaris Plage

Quartier Acotz, 720 route des Plages, F-64500 Saint Jean-de-Luz (Pyrénées-Atlantiques)
t: **05 59 26 55 90** e: **tamaris1@wanadoo.fr**
alanrogers.com/FR64080 www.tamaris-plage.com

Accommodation: ☑Pitch ☑Mobile home/chalet ☐Hotel/B&B ☐Apartment

This is a popular, small and pleasant site which is well kept. It is situated outside the town and just across the road from a sandy beach. The 35 touring pitches, all with 7/10A electricity, are of a good size and separated by hedges, on slightly sloping ground with some shade. The site becomes full for July and August with families on long stays, so a reservation then is essential. Mobile homes for rent occupy a further 40 pitches. A leisure centre and club provides a heated pool and various other free facilities for adults and children. A gym, Turkish bath, massage and other relaxing amenities are available at an extra charge. There is no shop, but bread is available daily across the road. Opposite the site there is a popular surf school that offers instruction to both new and experienced surfers.

You might like to know
Spain is just 20 km. away - great for a day trip!

☑ **Dogs welcome** *(subject to conditions)*
☑ **Dogs welcome all season**
☐ **Dogs welcome part season**
☐ **Breed restrictions**
(e.g. only small dogs accepted)
☐ **Number restrictions** *(max. 1 or 2 dogs)*
☑ **Dog sanitary facilities**
(e.g. waste bins, bags)
☑ **Dog showers**
☑ **On-site dog walking area**
☐ **Kennels**
☑ **Vet nearby**
(able to help with UK Pet Passports)

Facilities: The single toilet block of good quality and unusual design should be an ample provision. Facilities for disabled visitors. Washing machine. Wellness health club with free facilities: swimming pool, TV and play room, club for children (4-11 yrs) and on payment: gym, Turkish bath and other health facilities, sunbathing area, jacuzzi, adult TV lounge. Off site: Beach, fishing, surfing 30 m. Bicycle hire and golf 4 km. Riding 7 km.

Open: All year.

Directions: Proceed south on N10 and 1.5 km. after Guethary take the first road on the right (before access to the motorway and Carrefour centre commercial) and follow site signs. GPS: 43.41794, -1.62399

Charges guide

Per unit incl. 2 persons and electricity	€ 17,00 - € 29,00
extra person (over 2 yrs)	€ 5,00 - € 7,00
dog	€ 6,00

Chadotel Camping le Roussillon

Cami á la Mar, F-66750 Saint Cyprien (Pyrénées-Orientales)
t: 04 68 21 06 45   e: info@chadotel.com
alanrogers.com/FR66210   www.chadotel.com

Accommodation: ☑Pitch ☑Mobile home/chalet ☐ Hotel/B&B ☐ Apartment

This a comfortable site, although perhaps somewhat lacking in character. It is part of the Chadotel Group and has a quiet situation on the edge of St Cyprien village, some 2 km. from the beach. A bus service runs in the main season. The site benefits from having a good sized, traditionally shaped swimming pool, with the added attraction for children of a water slide, and plenty of sunbathing areas for adults. There are 150 pitches on the site with only 30 well kept, grassy, level touring pitches. Of a good size, they all have 6A electricity connections.

You might like to know
This site is well located for visiting the historic city of Perpignan, and the many delightful Catalan villages in the area.

☑ **Dogs welcome** (subject to conditions)

☑ **Dogs welcome all season**

☐ **Dogs welcome part season**

☐ **Breed restrictions**
(e.g. only small dogs accepted)

☑ **Number restrictions** (max. 1 or 2 dogs)

☐ **Dog sanitary facilities**
(e.g. waste bins, bags)

☐ **Dog showers**

☐ **On-site dog walking area**

☐ **Kennels**

☐ **Vet nearby**
(able to help with UK Pet Passports)

Facilities: Two toilet blocks (one older but refurbished, one more modern) provide modern facilities including a baby bath, laundry and facilities for disabled visitors. Shop. Bar/snack bar with terrace and entertainment in season. New takeaway. Play area on grass. Refurbished swimming pool, good sunbathing area and children's pool. Bicycle hire.

Open: 3 April - 25 September.

Directions: From D81 southwards (don't enter St Cyprien Plage), follow signs for Argelès. At roundabout ('Aqualand' signed to the left) turn right towards St Cyprien village. Bear right, site is indicated by large Chadotel sign on the right. GPS: 42.61878, 3.01596

Charges guide

Per unit incl. 2 persons and electricity	€ 18,50 - € 31,00

FRANCE – Font-Romeu

Huttopia Font-Romeu

Route de Mont-Louis, F-66120 Font-Romeu (Pyrénées-Orientales)
t: 04 68 30 09 32 e: font-romeu@huttopia.com
alanrogers.com/FR66250 www.huttopia.com

Accommodation: ☑Pitch ☑Mobile home/chalet ☐ Hotel/B&B ☐ Apartment

This is a large, open site of some seven hectares, nestling on the side of the mountain at the entrance to Font-Romeu. This part of the Pyrénées offers some staggering views and the famous Mont Louis is close by. An ideal base for climbing, hiking or cycling, it would also provide a good stopover for a night or so whilst travelling between Spain and France or to or from Andorra into France. The terraced pitches are easily accessed, with those dedicated to caravans and motorcaravans at the top of the site, whilst tents are on the lower slopes. Trees provide shade to many of the pitches from the sun which can be quite hot at this altitude. Facilities on site are limited to very good toilet blocks and a large games room and assembly hall which is used by those in tents when it rains.

You might like to know
Font-Romeu is one of Frances oldest skiing resorts, and also home to the worlds largest solar furnace!

☑ **Dogs welcome** (subject to conditions)
☑ **Dogs welcome all season**
☐ **Dogs welcome part season**
☐ **Breed restrictions**
  (e.g. only small dogs accepted)
☑ **Number restrictions** (max. 1 or 2 dogs)
☐ **Dog sanitary facilities**
  (e.g. waste bins, bags)
☐ **Dog showers**
☐ **On-site dog walking area**
☐ **Kennels**
☐ **Vet nearby**
  (able to help with UK Pet Passports)

Facilities: Two toilet blocks, one behind reception, the other in the centre of the tent pitches. Traditional in style, they are bright and clean with modern fittings. Toilet for children and excellent facilities for disabled visitors. Washing machines and dryers at each block. Large games hall. Only gas barbecues are permitted. Max. 1 dog. Off site: Opportunities for walking and climbing are close by as are golf, riding, fishing, cycling and tennis. The small town of Font-Romeu is very near with all the usual shops and banking facilities.

Open: 12 June - 19 September and 18 December - 2 April.

Directions: Font-Romeu is on the D118, some 12 km. after it branches off the N116 heading west, just after Mont Louis. This is an interesting road with magnificent views and well worth the climb. The site is just before the town, on the left and accessed off the car park.
GPS: 42.51511, 2.05183

Charges guide

Per unit incl. 2 persons

and electricity	€ 20,15 - € 28,55
extra person	€ 5,00 - € 6,30
child (2-7 yrs)	€ 3,00 - € 4,30
dog	€ 4,00

Images credit: R. Etie

70

FRANCE – Bassemberg

Campéole le Giessen

Route de Villé, F-67220 Bassemberg (Bas-Rhin)
t: 03 88 58 98 14   e: giessen@campeole.com
alanrogers.com/FR67070   www.campeole.com

Accommodation: ☑Pitch ☑Mobile home/chalet ☐Hotel/B&B ☐Apartment

Le Giessen is a member of the Campéole group and can be found at the foot of the Vosges mountains, with easy access to many of the best loved sights in Alsace. Although there is no pool on site, a large complex, comprising an indoor and outdoor pool with a water slide, can be found adjacent to the site, with free admission for all campers. Pitches here are grassy and of a good size, mostly with electrical connections. A number of mobile homes and fully equipped tents are available for rent. Various activities are organised in high season including a children's club and disco evenings. Nearby places of interest include the magnificent fortified castle of Haut-Koenigsbourg, as well as the great cities of Strasbourg and Colmar. This is a good base for exploring the Vosges and the Route du Vin (bicycle hire in the village). The site's friendly managers will be pleased to recommend possible itineraries.

Facilities: Multisport court. Bar. Play area. Activities and entertainment. Tourist information. Mobile homes and equipped tents for rent. Off site: Swimming pool complex adjacent. Tennis. Rollerblading rink. Hiking and mountain biking. Bicycle hire. Riding. Strasbourg 50 km.

Open: 1 April - 18 September.

Directions: Leave the A35 autoroute at exit 17 (Villé) and follow the D697 to Villé. Continue south on D39 to Bassemberg from where the site is well indicated. GPS: 48.33722, 7.28862

Charges guide

Per unit incl. 2 persons and electricity	€ 15,10 - € 24,50

You might like to know
Some lovely walks close to this site. Dogs must be kept on a lead on site.

- ☑ **Dogs welcome** *(subject to conditions)*
- ☑ **Dogs welcome all season**
- ☐ **Dogs welcome part season**
- ☑ **Breed restrictions** *(e.g. only small dogs accepted)*
- ☑ **Number restrictions** *(max. 1 or 2 dogs)*
- ☐ **Dog sanitary facilities** *(e.g. waste bins, bags)*
- ☐ **Dog showers**
- ☐ **On-site dog walking area**
- ☐ **Kennels**
- ☐ **Vet nearby** *(able to help with UK Pet Passports)*

Campéole la Nublière

30 allée de la Nublière, F-74210 Doussard (Haute-Savoie)
t: 04 50 44 33 44 e: nubliere@wanadoo.fr
alanrogers.com/FR74190 www.campeole.com

Accommodation: ☑Pitch ☑Mobile home/chalet ☐Hotel/B&B ☐Apartment

If you are looking for large pitches, shady trees, mountain views and direct access to the lakeside beach, this site is for you. There are 271 touring pitches of which 243 have electrical hook-ups (6A). This area is very popular and the site is very likely to be busy in high season. There may be some noise from the road and the public beach. La Nublière is 16 km. from old Annecy and you are spoilt for choice in how to get there. Take a ferry trip, hire a sailing boat or pedalo, or walk or cycle along the traffic free track towards the town. The local beach and sailing club are close and there is a good restaurant on the site perimeter. Across the road from the site are courts for tennis and boules. The site is perfect for walking, cycling or sailing and in low season provides a tranquil base for those just wishing to relax in natural surroundings on the edge of a nature reserve.

You might like to know
Some great walks in the area. Dogs must be kept on a lead on site.

☑ **Dogs welcome** *(subject to conditions)*
☑ **Dogs welcome all season**
☐ **Dogs welcome part season**
☑ **Breed restrictions**
(e.g. only small dogs accepted)
☑ **Number restrictions** *(max. 1 or 2 dogs)*
☐ **Dog sanitary facilities**
(e.g. waste bins, bags)
☐ **Dog showers**
☐ **On-site dog walking area**
☐ **Kennels**
☐ **Vet nearby**
(able to help with UK Pet Passports)

Facilities: Large clean sanitary blocks include free hot showers and good facilities for disabled visitors. Laundry. Shop (1/5-15/9). Restaurant on site perimeter (closed Mondays). Children's club (3/7-26/8) for 4-8 yrs. Safe deposit. Off site: Small supermarket adjacent to site. Good watersports area within 70 m. Access to town beach from site. Fishing 100 m. Golf and riding 4 km. Bicycle hire 7 km.

Open: 28 April - 18 September.

Directions: Site is 16 km. south of Annecy on Route d'Albertville, well signed.
GPS: 45.7908, 6.2197

Charges guide

Per unit incl. 2 persons and electricity	€ 17,10 - € 26,60
extra person	€ 4,50 - € 6,80
child (2-6 yrs)	free - € 4,30

Campéole La Pinède

F-74140 Excenevex Plage (Haute-Savoie)
t: 04 50 72 85 05 e: pinede@campeole.com
alanrogers.com/FR74280 www.campeole.com

Accommodation: ☑ Pitch ☑ Mobile home/chalet ☐ Hotel/B&B ☐ Apartment

La Pinède is a member of the Campéole group and has direct access to Excenevex beach, the only naturally sandy beach on Lake Geneva. The site has a pleasant woodland setting and pitches are of a good size, all with electricity (10A). Mobile homes, chalets and fully equipped tents are available for rent (including specially adapted units for wheelchair users). There is a supervised bathing area on the beach, which shelves gradually, and a small harbour (suitable only for boats with a shallow draught). Other amenities include a shop and takeaway food service, as well as an entertainment marquee and children's play area. There is plenty of activity here in high season with a children's club and regular discos and karaoke evenings. Geneva is just 25 km. distant and other possible excursions include Thonon-les-Bains with its weekly market and, of course, boat trips on Lake Geneva. Dramatic mountain scenery is close at hand, notably the spectacular Dent d'Oche (2,222 m) and the Gorges du Pont du Diable.

You might like to know
Some nice walks along the banks of Lake Geneva. All dogs to be kept on a lead on the campsite.

☑ **Dogs welcome** *(subject to conditions)*
☑ **Dogs welcome all season**
☐ **Dogs welcome part season**
☑ **Breed restrictions**
   (e.g. only small dogs accepted)
☑ **Number restrictions** *(max. 1 or 2 dogs)*
☐ **Dog sanitary facilities**
   (e.g. waste bins, bags)
☐ **Dog showers**
☐ **On-site dog walking area**
☐ **Kennels**
☐ **Vet nearby**
   (able to help with UK Pet Passports)

Facilities: Lake beach. Takeaway food. Play area. Bouncy castle. Activities and entertainment programme. Tourist information. Mobile homes, chalets and equipped tents for rent. Off site: Geneva 25 km. Thonon-les-Bains 15 km. Hiking and cycle tracks. Riding. Golf

Open: 11 April - 11 September.

Directions: From Geneva head along the south side of the lake on the D1005 as far as Massongy and shortly beyond here take the northbound D324 to Escenevex. The site is well indicated from here. GPS: 46.34492, 6.35808

Charges guide

Per unit incl. 2 persons and electricity	€ 17,10 - € 26,60

FRANCE – Rambouillet

Huttopia Rambouillet

Rue du Château d'Eau, F-78120 Rambouillet (Yvelines)
t: 01 30 41 07 34   e: rambouillet@huttopia.com
alanrogers.com/FR78040   www.huttopia.com

Accommodation: ☑Pitch ☑Mobile home/chalet ☐ Hotel/B&B ☐ Apartment

This pleasant site is now part of the Huttopia group whose philosophy is to 'rediscover the camping spirit'. It is in a peaceful forest location beside a lake, with good tarmac access roads and site lighting. The 190 touring pitches, 150 with electrical connections, are set among the trees and in clearings. As a result, shade is plentiful and grass sparse. The main area is kept traffic-free but there is a section for motorcaravans and those who need or prefer to have their car with them. The result is a safe, child-friendly site. There is an 'espace nature' with 40 huge pitches for campers. As part of their efforts to be environmentally friendly, Huttopia have built a 'Natural Swimming Pool'. The water is filtered by reeds and it was used for the first time in 2008 and passed the stringent tests of France's Ministry of Health. From your pitch, you can stroll out into the forest and there are many good cycle routes and footpaths in the area. Rambouillet itself is an interesting town and Chartres and Versailles are within easy reach. It is possible to visit Paris by rail (a 30 minute journey).

You might like to know
This site is located within a vast forest - watch out for the deer and wild boar!

- ☑ **Dogs welcome** *(subject to conditions)*
- ☑ **Dogs welcome all season**
- ☐ **Dogs welcome part season**
- ☐ **Breed restrictions**
  (e.g. only small dogs accepted)
- ☑ **Number restrictions** *(max. 1 or 2 dogs)*
- ☐ **Dog sanitary facilities**
  (e.g. waste bins, bags)
- ☐ **Dog showers**
- ☑ **On-site dog walking area**
- ☐ **Kennels**
- ☐ **Vet nearby**
  (able to help with UK Pet Passports)

Facilities: The brand new sanitary block has controllable showers, some washbasins in cubicles and a number of more spacious 'family' cubicles. Facilities for disabled visitors. Laundry facilities. Three outlying 'rondavels' each with two family rooms. Motorcaravan service point. Small shop selling basics plus bar/restaurant with terrace (July-Aug and weekends). Games room with TV. Free internet and WiFi. Play area. 'Natural' swimming pool (June-Sept). Bicycle hire. Fishing. Family activities with a 'natural' theme (July-Aug). No American motorhomes or twin-axle caravans. Off site: Riding 5 km. Lake with beach 10 km. Golf 15 km.

Open: 4 April - 5 November.

Directions: Site is southeast of town: from N10 southbound take Rambouillet/Les Eveuses exit, northbound take Rambouillet centre exit, loop round (site signed) and rejoin N10 southbound, taking next exit. Pass under N10, following signs to site in 1.7 km. GPS: 48.62638, 1.84375

Charges guide

Per unit incl. 2 persons and electricity	€ 17,50 - € 26,20
extra person	€ 5,50 - € 6,90
child (2-7 yrs)	€ 3,00 - € 4,30
dog	€ 4,00

Images credit: R. Etie

FRANCE – Agay

Camping Caravaning Esterel

Avenue des Golf, Agay, F-83530 Saint Raphaël (Var)
t: 04 94 82 03 28   e: contact@esterel-caravaning.fr
alanrogers.com/FR83020   www.esterel-caravaning.fr

Accommodation: ☑Pitch ☑Mobile home/chalet ☐Hotel/B&B ☐Apartment

Esterel is a quality caravan site east of St Raphaël, set among the hills behind Agay. The site is 3.5 km. from the sandy beach at Agay where parking is perhaps a little easier than at most places on this coast. It has 230 pitches for tourers, for caravans but not tents; all have electricity and water tap, 18 special ones have their own en-suite washroom adjoining. Pitches are on shallow terraces, attractively landscaped with good shade and a variety of flowers, giving a feeling of spaciousness. Some 'maxi-pitches' from 110 to 160 m². are available with 10A electricity. Developed by the Laroche family for over 30 years, the site has an attractive, quiet situation with good views of the Esterel mountains. Wild boar occasionally come to the perimeter fence to be fed by visitors. This is a very good site, well run and organised in a deservedly popular area. A pleasant courtyard area contains the shop and bar, with a terrace overlooking the attractively landscaped (floodlit at night) pool complex.

You might like to know
There are some fine walks through the Esterel forest park - watch out for wild boars though!

☑ **Dogs welcome** (subject to conditions)
☑ **Dogs welcome all season**
☐ **Dogs welcome part season**
☐ **Breed restrictions**
   (e.g. only small dogs accepted)
☑ **Number restrictions** (max. 1 or 2 dogs)
☐ **Dog sanitary facilities**
   (e.g. waste bins, bags)
☐ **Dog showers**
☐ **On-site dog walking area**
☐ **Kennels**
☐ **Vet nearby**
   (able to help with UK Pet Passports)

Facilities: Excellent refurbished, heated toilet blocks. Individual toilet units on 18 pitches. Facilities for disabled visitors. Laundry room. Motorcaravan services. Shop. Gift shop. Takeaway. Bar/restaurant. Five circular swimming pools (two heated), one for adults, one for children (covered and heated), three arranged as a waterfall (all season). Spa with sauna etc. Disco. Archery. Minigolf. Tennis. Pony rides. Petanque. Squash. Playground. Nursery. Bicycle hire. Internet access. Organised events in season. No barbecues. Off site: Golf nearby. Trekking by foot, bicycle or pony in L'Esterel forest park. Fishing, beach 3 km.

Open: 27 March - 2 October.

Directions: From A8, exit Fréjus, follow signs for Valescure, then for Agay, site on left. The road from Agay is the easiest to follow but it is possible to approach from St Raphaël via Valescure. GPS: 43.453775, 6.832817

Charges guide

Per unit incl. 2 persons	
and electricity	€ 18,00 - € 60,00
extra person	€ 9,00
child (1-7 yrs)	€ 7,00
dog	€ 2,00

FRANCE – Saint Aygulf

Camping Résidence du Campeur

B.P. 12, D7, F-83371 Saint Aygulf (Var)
t: 04 94 81 01 59 e: info@residence-campeur.com
alanrogers.com/FR83050 www.residence-campeur.com

Accommodation: ☑Pitch ☑Mobile home/chalet ☐Hotel/B&B ☐Apartment

This excellent site near the Côte d'Azur will take you away from all the bustle of the Mediterranean coast. Spread out over ten hectares, there are separate areas for mobile homes and touring caravans and tents, with pitches arranged along avenues. The 67 touring pitches average 100 m². in size and all have electricity connections and private sanitary facilities (although washbasins double as dishwashing sinks). The bar/restaurant is surrounded by a shady terrace, whilst friendly staff provide an excellent service. A pleasant pool complex is available for those who wish to stay on site instead of going swimming in the nearby lake or from the Mediterranean beaches. Activities are organised daily during the summer season and the site has its own open air cinema.

You might like to know
The site has an extensive aqua park yet is only 2.5 km. from the sandy Côte d'Azur beaches. Inland there are opportunities for rambling and mountain biking.

☑ **Dogs welcome** *(subject to conditions)*
☑ **Dogs welcome all season**
☐ **Dogs welcome part season**
☐ **Breed restrictions**
   (e.g. only small dogs accepted)
☑ **Number restrictions** *(max. 1 or 2 dogs)*
☐ **Dog sanitary facilities**
   (e.g. waste bins, bags)
☐ **Dog showers**
☐ **On-site dog walking area**
☐ **Kennels**
☐ **Vet nearby**
   (able to help with UK Pet Passports)

Facilities: Private toilet blocks are cleaned at regular intervals and include a washbasin, shower and WC. Laundry area with washing machines. Well stocked supermarket. Bar/restaurant. Takeaway (all open all season). New swimming pool complex with four water slides (high season). Two tennis courts. Minigolf. Boules. Fishing. Bicycle hire. Play area. Games/TV room. Only gas or electric barbecues are permitted. Off site: Riding 1.5 km. Golf 2 km. Beach and St Aygulf 2.5 km. Water skiing nearby.

Open: 27 March - 30 September.

Directions: Leave A8 at Le Muy exit (no. 36) on N555 towards Draguignan then onto the N7 towards Fréjus. Turn right on D7 signed St Aygulf and site is on the right about 2.5 km. before the town. GPS: 43.40905, 6.70893

Charges guide

Per unit incl. 3 persons and electricity	€ 30,10 - € 50,15
extra person	€ 5,19 - € 8,65
child (under 7 yrs)	€ 3,54 - € 5,90
dog	€ 4,00

FRANCE – Roquebrune-sur-Argens

Kawan Village les Pêcheurs

F-83520 Roquebrune-sur-Argens (Var)
t: 04 94 45 71 25 e: info@camping-les-pecheurs.com
alanrogers.com/FR83200 www.camping-les-pecheurs.com

Accommodation: ☑Pitch ☑Mobile home/chalet ☐ Hotel/B&B ☐ Apartment

Les Pêcheurs will appeal to families who appreciate natural surroundings together with many activities, cultural and sporting. Interspersed with mobile homes, the 150 good sized touring pitches (6/10A electricity) are separated by trees or flowering bushes. The Provencal style buildings are delightful, especially the bar, restaurant and games room, with its terrace down to the river and the site's own canoe station (locked gate). Across the road is a lake used exclusively for water skiing with a sandy beach, a restaurant and minigolf. Enlarged spa facilities include a swimming pool, large jacuzzi, massage, steam pool and a sauna. Developed over three generations by the Simoncini family, this peaceful, friendly site is set in more than four hectares of mature, well shaded countryside at the foot of the Roquebrune Rock. Activities include climbing the 'Rock' with a guide. The Rock and the Holy Hole, the Three Crosses and the Hermit all call for further exploration which reception staff are happy to arrange, likewise trips to Monte Carlo, Ventimigua (Italy) and the Gorges du Verdon, etc.

You might like to know
Natural setting beside a river and opposite a lake. Shady pitches available; maximum 1 dog per pitch.

☑ **Dogs welcome** *(subject to conditions)*
☑ **Dogs welcome all season**
☐ **Dogs welcome part season**
☐ **Breed restrictions**
  (e.g. only small dogs accepted)
☐ **Number restrictions** *(max. 1 or 2 dogs)*
☐ **Dog sanitary facilities**
  (e.g. waste bins, bags)
☐ **Dog showers**
☐ **On-site dog walking area**
☐ **Kennels**
☐ **Vet nearby**
  (able to help with UK Pet Passports)

Facilities: Modern, refurbished, well designed toilet blocks, baby baths, facilities for disabled visitors. Washing machines. Shop. Bar and restaurant (all open all season). Heated outdoor swimming pool (all season), separate paddling pool (lifeguard in high season), ice cream bar. Games room. Spa facilities. Playing field. Fishing. Canoeing. Waterskiing. Rafting and diving schools. Activities for children and adults (high season), visits to local wine caves. Only gas or electric barbecues. WiFi in reception, bar/restaurant and pool area. Off site: Bicycle hire 1 km. Riding 5 km. Golf 5 km (reduced fees).

Open: 1 April - 30 September.

Directions: From A8 take Le Muy exit, follow the N7 towards Fréjus for 13 km. bypassing Le Muy. After crossing A8, turn right at roundabout towards Roquebrune-sur-Argens. Site is on left after 1 km. just before bridge over river. GPS: 43.450783, 6.6335

Charges guide

Per unit incl. 2 persons and electricity	€ 23,00 - € 43,00
extra person	€ 4,00 - € 7,80
child (5-10 yrs)	€ 3,20 - € 6,20
dog (max. 1)	€ 3,20

Chadotel Camping l'Océano d'Or

58 rue Georges Clémenceau, B.P. 12, F-85520 Jard-sur-Mer (Vendée)
t: 02 51 33 05 05 e: info@chadotel.com
alanrogers.com/FR85270 www.chadotel.com

Accommodation: ☑ Pitch ☑ Mobile home/chalet ☐ Hotel/B&B ☐ Apartment

This site should appeal to families with children of all ages. It is very lively in high season but appears to be well managed, with a full programme of activities (it can therefore be noisy, sometimes late at night). The site is only 1 km. from the excellent beach. There are 430 flat, grass and sand pitches of which 40% are occupied by tour operators and mobile homes. The 260 for touring units, all with 6A electricity, are quite large (about 100 m²). Some are separated by high hedges, others are more open with low bushes between them. There are shops, bars and restaurants, and a weekly market in the pleasant little town of Jard-sur-Mer.

You might like to know

Footpaths and bicycle routes lead you through pine forests and down to the beach. Close to the protected environmental areas of the Marais de Talmont.

☑ **Dogs welcome** *(subject to conditions)*
☑ **Dogs welcome all season**
☐ **Dogs welcome part season**
☐ **Breed restrictions**
  (e.g. only small dogs accepted)
☑ **Number restrictions** *(max. 1 or 2 dogs)*
☐ **Dog sanitary facilities**
  (e.g. waste bins, bags)
☐ **Dog showers**
☐ **On-site dog walking area**
☐ **Kennels**
☐ **Vet nearby**
  (able to help with UK Pet Passports)

Facilities: Four rather dated, unisex toilet blocks include washbasins all in cabins (cleaning and maintenance is variable). Dishwashing and laundry facilities. Shop (1/6-10/9). Bar and snack bar (1/6-10/9, limited hours outside high season). Swimming pool (heated 20/5-20/9) with slides, waterfalls and children's pool. Walled (three sides) play area. Tennis. Pétanque. Minigolf. Electric barbecues are not allowed. Max. 1 dog.
Off site: Excellent beach within walking distance. Golf, riding, karting and other activities within 15 km.

Open: 9 April - 25 September.

Directions: Site is on the D21 Talmont-St Hilaire - Longeville sur Mer, just east of the turning to the town centre. GPS: 46.42075, -1.5694

Charges guide

Per unit incl. 2 persons and electricity	€ 15,40 - € 29,90

FRANCE – Bretignolles-sur-Mer

Chadotel Camping la Trévillière

1 Rue de Bellevue, F-85470 Bretignolles-sur-Mer (Vendée)
t: **02 51 90 09 65** e: **info@chadotel.com**
alanrogers.com/FR85310 www.chadotel.com

Accommodation: ☑Pitch ☑Mobile home/chalet ☐ Hotel/B&B ☐ Apartment

In a pleasant rural setting, la Trévillière is on the edge of the little resort town of Bretignolles. There are 200 pitches, 110 for tourers, all with access to water and electricity (long leads required in places). Some are level, some sloping; all are separated by hedges or low bushes either with shade or more open. Although just 2 km. from the nearest beach and less than 5 km. from the Plage des Dunes (one of southern Vendée's best beaches), la Trévillière has a more 'laid-back' feel than many other sites in the area, particularly in low season. There is a heated swimming pool with water slide, a small paddling pool and a large sunbathing terrace with plenty of loungers, one part has a retractable cover. Overlooking the pool is the building housing the bar and reception. In early season the site is very quiet, becoming much livelier in July and August when there is a good range of morning activities for children, afternoon events for families and evening entertainment for all. The site has over 60 mobile homes and chalets, half available for rent, and is used by one small French tour operator.

You might like to know
Walking routes and bicycle paths through the dunes of Sauzaie and the Valley of Jaunay with its 45 km. lake and protected habitats.

☑ **Dogs welcome** *(subject to conditions)*
☑ **Dogs welcome all season**
☐ **Dogs welcome part season**
☐ **Breed restrictions**
  (e.g. only small dogs accepted)
☑ **Number restrictions** *(max. 1 or 2 dogs)*
☐ **Dog sanitary facilities**
  (e.g. waste bins, bags)
☐ **Dog showers**
☐ **On-site dog walking area**
☐ **Kennels**
☐ **Vet nearby**
  (able to help with UK Pet Passports)

Facilities: Three traditional toilet blocks, a little tired in parts, include washbasins in cubicles, pushbutton showers, a unit for disabled visitors and a baby room with bath, shower and toilet. Warm water for dishwashing and laundry sinks. Washing machines and dryers. Bar (1/5-30/9). Small shop (15/6-10/9). Snack bar with takeaway (1/6-10/9). Heated pool with slide and paddling pool. Play area. Minigolf. Max. 1 dog.
Off site: Shops, restaurants and bars 1 km. Beach 2 km. Fishing, sailing and riding all 3 km. Golf 10 km.

Open: 3 April - 1 November.

Directions: From north, after St Gilles go through Bretignolles-La Sauzaie (left fork) and before reaching Bretignolles turn left on sharp right hand bend, heading for water tower. Site on right in 800 m. From south, after Bretignolles, turn right (sign Ecoles), then left. Site signed to left after stadium. GPS: 46.63632, -1.85844

Charges guide

Per unit incl. 2 persons and electricity	€ 15,40 - € 29,50
extra person	€ 5,80
child (2-13 yrs)	€ 3,80
dog	€ 3,00

FRANCE – Saint Vincent-sur-Jard

Chadotel Camping la Bolée d'Air

Route de Bouil, F-85520 Saint Vincent-sur-Jard (Vendée)
t: 02 51 90 36 05 e: info@chadotel.com
alanrogers.com/FR85430 www.chadotel.com

Accommodation: ☑Pitch ☑Mobile home/chalet ☐Hotel/B&B ☐Apartment

This is a well managed site with good facilities and a varied programme of high season entertainment just 900 m. away from a sandy beach. The 120 touring pitches are all level and well grassed on sandy soil. Many are situated around the perimeter and separated by hedges, giving good privacy but little shade. Long electricity cables may be required on some. The main road runs along one side of the site and may cause traffic noise at times, although when we visited in July there did not appear to be a problem. The site is used by two small tour operators. A refurbished complex at the entrance houses all the amenities. The village of St Vincent-sur-Jard (1.5 km) has shops, bars and restaurants and the pleasant seaside town of Jard-sur-Mer with its market is just 3.5 km. away.

You might like to know
A pine forest separates the campsite from the long sandy beach and offers pedestrian walkways and cycle routes.

☑ **Dogs welcome** (subject to conditions)
☑ **Dogs welcome all season**
☐ **Dogs welcome part season**
☐ **Breed restrictions**
    (e.g. only small dogs accepted)
☐ **Number restrictions** (max. 1 or 2 dogs)
☐ **Dog sanitary facilities**
    (e.g. waste bins, bags)
☐ **Dog showers**
☐ **On-site dog walking area**
☐ **Kennels**
☐ **Vet nearby**
    (able to help with UK Pet Passports)

Facilities: Three modernised, unisex toilet blocks provide washbasins in cabins, plenty of sinks for dishwashing and laundry, washing machines and dryers. Shop and takeaway (1/6-31/8). Bar (1/5-30/9). Heated indoor pool, outdoor pool (1/6-30/9) with slide, jacuzzi and paddling pool. Tennis. Minigolf. Bicycle hire. Good multi-sport all-weather terrain. Off site: Beach 900 m. Bus service in town. Karting and other activities within 1.5 km. Riding 4 km. Fishing 10 km.

Open: 3 April - 25 September.

Directions: Site is just off the D21 Les Sables La Franche road, just east of St Vincent-sur-Jard and is well signed from the main road.
GPS: 46.41839, -1.52791

Charges guide

Per unit incl. 2 persons and electricity	€ 15,40 - € 29,50

Cofton Country Holidays

Starcross, Dawlish EX6 8RP (Devon)
t: **01626 890111** e: **info@coftonholidays.co.uk**
alanrogers.com/UK0970 www.coftonholidays.co.uk

Accommodation: ☑Pitch ☑Mobile home/chalet ☐ Hotel/B&B ☐ Apartment

A popular, family run park, Cofton is 1.5 miles from a sandy beach at Dawlish Warren. It has space for 450 touring units on a variety of fields and meadows with beautiful country views. The smaller, more mature fields, including a pleasant old orchard for tents only, are well terraced. While there are terraces on most of the slopes of the larger, more open fields, there are still some quite steep gradients to climb. There are some 450 electrical connections (10A), 16 hardstandings and 14 'super' pitches. One area has 66 park-owned holiday homes for let. A well designed, central complex overlooking the pool and decorated with flowers and hanging baskets, houses reception, a shop and off-licence and a bar lounge, the 'Cofton Swan', where bar meals are available (all Easter-end October). A family room and bar are on the first floor of this building and there is an outdoor terrace and some light entertainment in season. The adjacent supervised, kidney-shaped, heated pool with paddling pool, has lots of grassy space for sunbathing. Coarse fishing is available in five lakes on the park.

You might like to know

There is a special dog walking area on site, and many walks in the surrounding countryside.

☑ **Dogs welcome** (subject to conditions)
☑ **Dogs welcome all season**
☐ **Dogs welcome part season**
☐ **Breed restrictions**
   (e.g. only small dogs accepted)
☑ **Number restrictions** (max. 1 or 2 dogs)
☐ **Dog sanitary facilities**
   (e.g. waste bins, bags)
☐ **Dog showers**
☑ **On-site dog walking area**
☐ **Kennels**
☐ **Vet nearby**
   (able to help with UK Pet Passports)

Facilities: Toilet facilities comprise six blocks, well placed for all areas, one of very high standard. Facilities for disabled visitors and babies. Hair dryers. Two launderettes. Gas available. Ice pack hire service. Bar lounge. TV. Shop. Fish and chip shop also serving breakfast. Swimming pool (overall length 100 ft. open Spr.B.H-mid Sept). Games room. Adventure playground in the woods overlooking the pools and two other well equipped play areas. Coarse fishing (from £ 25 per rod for 7 days, discount for senior citizens outside July/Aug). Caravan storage. Seasonal pitches. Off site: Beach 1.5 miles. Woodland walks/pub 0.5 miles. Golf 3 miles.

Open: All year.

Directions: Access to the park is off the A379 road 3 miles north of Dawlish, just after Cockwood harbour village.
GPS: 50.6126, -3.460467

Charges guide

Per unit incl. 2 persons and electricity	£ 13,00 - £ 27,50
hardstanding pitch	£ 16,50 - £ 29,50
serviced pitch	£ 19,50 - £ 33,50
extra person (over 2 yrs)	£ 2,50 - £ 4,75

Golden Sands Holiday Park

Week Lane, Dawlish Warren EX7 0LZ (Devon)
t: **01626 863099**
alanrogers.com/UK1085 www.parkholidaysuk.com

Accommodation: ☑Pitch ☑Mobile home/chalet ☐ Hotel/B&B ☐ Apartment

Dawlish is a deservedly popular South Devon resort. Golden Sands is one of three Park Holidays sites in this area. There is some up and down walking to access a good range of facilities. There are only 28 touring pitches at Golden Sands, most with 16A electricity. Accommodation is mainly provided in mobile homes and chalets for rent. Evening entertainment is to a high standard and is organised nightly in peak season. Leisure facilities include indoor and covered swimming pools and an amusement arcade. There is also a dining area (with takeaway food). Dawlish Warren can be accessed on foot and is home to an important nature reserve. The Warren is the main roost for the wildfowl and wading birds of the Exe estuary. By way of contrast, Powderham Castle dates back over 600 years and is the historic home of the Earl of Devon. This part of Devon is well known for the quality of its beaches and there is a wide choice of fine sandy beaches close at hand.

Special offers

Golden Sands Holiday Park welcomes your four legged friends with plenty of walking facilities on the park for you both to stretch your legs! Prices are from £2 per dog per night.

You might like to know

Most dogs are welcome at our parks with a maximum of two dogs per booking. Some breeds of dog, including those listed in the Dangerous Dog Act 1991, are not allowed.

☑ **Dogs welcome** *(subject to conditions)*
☑ **Dogs welcome all season**
☐ **Dogs welcome part season**
☑ **Breed restrictions**
  (e.g. only small dogs accepted)
☑ **Number restrictions** *(max. 1 or 2 dogs)*
☑ **Dog sanitary facilities**
  (e.g. waste bins, bags)
☐ **Dog showers**
☑ **On-site dog walking area**
☐ **Kennels**
☑ **Vet nearby**
  (able to help with UK Pet Passports)

Facilities: Basic toilet block with washbasins and preset showers. Facilities for disabled visitors (but quite hilly ground to access). Laundry facilities. Shop. Bar. Restaurant. Indoor and outdoor swimming pools. Playground. Tourist information. Entertainment and activity programme (including children's club). Mobile homes and chalets for rent. Off site: Beach within walking distance. Golf 1 mile. Riding 4 miles. Dawlish (shops and restaurants). Crealy Adventure Park. Dawlish Warren.

Open: 1 March - 31 October.

Directions: Leave the M5 at exit 30 and take the A379 to Dawlish. Drive through Starcross and continue on the A379 for about 2 miles. Golden Sands is signed to the left 1 mile before reaching Dawlish. GPS: 50.596267, -3.456316

Charges guide

Per unit incl. 2 persons and electricity	£ 8,00 - £ 27,00

Peppermint Park

Warren Road, Dawlish Warren, Dawlish EX7 0PQ (Devon)
t: **01626 863436** e: **info@peppermintpark.co.uk**
alanrogers.com/UK1090 www.peppermintpark.co.uk

Accommodation: ☑Pitch ☑Mobile home/chalet ☐ Hotel/B&B ☐ Apartment

Now part of the Park Holidays group, Peppermint Park is a green oasis in a popular holiday area. Extensive, green, sloping fields edged with mature trees have been partly terraced to give level pitches for caravans and some more informal areas that cater for tents. There are 90 holiday homes (many privately owned but some to rent) along with timber lodges to rent, close to a small fishing lake. There are 75 touring pitches, 60 with 16A electricity, which are marked and numbered. Tarmac roads thread through the site giving easy access to all areas. Visitors staying at Peppermint Park can use all the facilities at nearby Dawlish Sands and Golden Sands, also part of the Park Holidays Group. Dawlish Warren's safe Blue Flag beaches and its associated pleasure complex are within walking distance (700 yds) making it ideal for families. For others, there is the adjacent coastal footpath or the city of Exeter (7 miles) with its cathedral, museums and historic Quay complex. A passenger ferry operates from Starcross (2 miles) across the estuary to Exmouth during high season.

Special offers
At Peppermint Park, we welcome your four legged friends - with prices starting from £2 per dog per night, who wouldn't want to take Rover on holiday with them!

You might like to know
Most dogs are welcome at our parks with a maximum of 2 dogs per booking. Some breeds of dog including those listed in the Dangerous Dogs Act 1991 are not allowed.

☑ **Dogs welcome** *(subject to conditions)*
☑ **Dogs welcome all season**
☐ **Dogs welcome part season**
☑ **Breed restrictions**
  (e.g. only small dogs accepted)
☑ **Number restrictions** *(max. 1 or 2 dogs)*
☑ **Dog sanitary facilities**
  (e.g. waste bins, bags)
☐ **Dog showers**
☑ **On-site dog walking area**
☐ **Kennels**
☑ **Vet nearby**
  (able to help with UK Pet Passports)

Facilities: Two fully equipped sanitary blocks can be heated. Two units (WC, washbasin and shower) for disabled visitors. Baby room. Laundry (washing machines, dryers and free irons). Shop with gas. Adventure playground on a hill. Field for ball games. Small coarse fishing lake (£5 for adult day ticket). WiFi throughout. Off site: Golf at Dawlish Warren (18-hole links course), 9-hole course at Starcross. Riding and bicycle hire 2 miles. Sailing and boat launching 5 miles.

Open: 1 March - 31 October.

Directions: Leave the M5 at exit 30 and take A379 Dawlish road. Pass through Starcross (7 miles) then turn left to Dawlish Warren just before Dawlish. Continue for 1.5 miles down hill and park is on left in 300 yards. GPS: 50.599367, -3.446967

Charges guide

Per unit incl. 2 persons and electricity	£ 8,00 - £ 27,00
extra person (2 yrs and over)	£ 2,00 - £ 4,00
dog	£ 2,00 - £ 4,00

Wareham Forest Tourist Park

North Trigon, Wareham BH20 7NZ (Dorset)
t: **01929 551393** e: **holiday@warehamforest.co.uk**
alanrogers.com/UK2030 www.warehamforest.co.uk

Accommodation: ☑Pitch ☑Mobile home/chalet ☐Hotel/B&B ☐Apartment

This peacefully located and spacious park, on the edge of Wareham Forest, has 200 pitches and is continually being upgraded by its enthusiastic owners, Tony and Sarah Birch. The focal point of the park is the modern reception and shop, located by the pools. Four main areas provide a wide choice of touring pitches from grass to hardstanding and luxury, all with 16A electricity. Tenters have their own choice of open field or pinewood. The site has provided direct access for walkers into the forest or the seven miles of the Sika cycle trail may be used. The lovely market town of Wareham is accessible by bike without having to use the roads. This park has an almost continental feel, with plenty of space. Even when it is busy, it is calm and peaceful in its forest setting. In low season you may be lucky enough to spot the herd of Sika deer which live in the forest. The park is well situated to explore the Dorset coast and Thomas Hardy country. A member of the Best of British Group.

You might like to know
A herd of sika deer live in the forest - please take care when exercising your dog.

☑ **Dogs welcome** *(subject to conditions)*
☑ **Dogs welcome all season**
☐ **Dogs welcome part season**
☐ **Breed restrictions**
  (e.g. only small dogs accepted)
☑ **Number restrictions** *(max. 1 or 2 dogs)*
☐ **Dog sanitary facilities**
  (e.g. waste bins, bags)
☐ **Dog showers**
☐ **On-site dog walking area**
☐ **Kennels**
☐ **Vet nearby**
  (able to help with UK Pet Passports)

Facilities: Two well maintained toilet blocks are of a good standard with some washbasins in cubicles for ladies. The block used in the winter months is centrally heated. Facilities for disabled visitors. Well equipped laundry rooms. Motorcaravan service point. Small licensed shop with gas. Swimming pool (60x20 ft), heated 20/5-15/9. Large adventure play area. Barrier closed 23.00-07.00. Resident wardens on site. Caravan storage. WiFi. Off site: Cycle trail and walking in the forest. Bicycle hire and golf 3 miles. Fishing 5 miles. Riding 8 miles.

Open: All year.

Directions: From A31 Bere Regis, follow the A35 towards Poole for 0.5 miles and site is well signed to the right for a further 1.5 miles towards Wareham. GPS: 50.721733, -2.156217

Charges guide

Per unit incl. 2 persons and electricity	£ 15,50 - £ 30,00
'superior' pitch fully serviced	£ 18,00 - £ 33,00
extra person	£ 3,00 - £ 5,00
child (5-15 yrs)	£ 2,00 - £ 3,75
dog	free - £ 1,75

Couples and families only.

Beacon Hill Touring Park

Blandford Road North, Poole BH16 6AB (Dorset)
t: **01202 631631** e: **bookings@beaconhilltouringpark.co.uk**
alanrogers.com/UK2180 www.beaconhilltouringpark.co.uk

Accommodation: ☑Pitch ☑Mobile home/chalet ☐ Hotel/B&B ☐ Apartment

Beacon Hill is located in a marvellous, natural environment of partly wooded heathland, with certain areas of designated habitation for protected species such as sand lizards and the Dartford Warbler, but there is also easy access to main routes. Wildlife ponds encourage dragonflies and other species, but fishing is also possible. Conservation is obviously important in such a special area but one can ramble at will over the 30 acres, with the hilltop walk a must. Grassy open spaces provide 170 pitches, 151 with 10A electricity, on sandy grass which is sometimes uneven. Of these, 50 are for tents only and a few are seasonal. The undulating nature of the land and the trees allows for discrete areas to be allocated for varying needs, for example young families near the play area, families with teenagers close to the bar/games room, those with dogs near the dog walking area, and young people further away. The park provides a wide range of facilities, including an open air swimming pool and a tennis court. It is well situated for beaches, Poole harbour and ferries for France or the Channel Isles.

Facilities: Two fully equipped toilet blocks include facilities for disabled people. Laundry facilities. Well stocked shop at reception. Coffee bar and takeaway (main season). Bar (July/Aug, B.Hs, half-terms). Heated swimming pool (mid May-mid Sept). All weather tennis court (charges). Adventure play areas including a hideaway. Games room with pool tables and amusement machines. TV room. Internet (WiFi). Fishing (charges). Off site: Poole harbour and ferries 3 miles. Riding 2 miles. Bicycle hire 3 miles. Brownsea Island, Studland beach with Sandbanks ferry and the Purbecks near.

Open: 17 March - end September.

Directions: Park is about 3 miles north of Poole. Take A350 (towards Blandford) at roundabout where A350 joins A35. Park signed to the right (northeast) after about 400 yards.
GPS: 50.74953, -2.03446

Special offers
Special discounts available.
Please visit website for details:
www.beaconhilltouringpark.co.uk.

You might like to know
The Park consists of 30 acres of partly wooded heathland hosting an abundance of wildlife and natural beauty. Certain areas are designated Special Areas of Conservation.

☑ **Dogs welcome** *(subject to conditions)*
☑ **Dogs welcome all season**
☐ **Dogs welcome part season**
☐ **Breed restrictions**
(e.g. only small dogs accepted)
☑ **Number restrictions** *(max. 1 or 2 dogs)*
☐ **Dog sanitary facilities**
(e.g. waste bins, bags)
☐ **Dog showers**
☐ **On-site dog walking area**
☐ **Kennels**
☐ **Vet nearby**
(able to help with UK Pet Passports)

Charges guide
Per unit incl. 2 persons and electricity	£ 13,50 - £ 35,00
extra person	£ 3,50 - £ 6,50
child (3-15 yrs)	£ 2,50 - £ 3,00
dog	£ 1,00 - £ 1,50

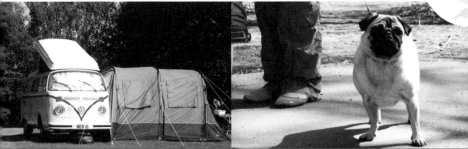

UNITED KINGDOM – Chichester

Chichester Lakeside Park

Vinnetrow Road, Chichester PO20 1QH (West Sussex)
t: 0845 815 9775 e: lakeside@ParkHolidays.com
alanrogers.com/UK2875 www.parkholidaysuk.com

Accommodation: ☑Pitch ☑Mobile home/chalet ☐Hotel/B&B ☐Apartment

Located just outside the historic city of Chichester, this large site is a member of the Park Holidays group. Please note that there are no touring pitches on this site. Accommodation is provided in a range of fully equipped mobile homes, available for rent. This is a mecca for anglers with no fewer than ten large fishing lakes. The site is set in 150 acres of Sussex countryside, but is also within easy access of a sandy beach and the traditional resort of Bognor Regis. This is a lively site in peak season with a newly refurbished entertainment centre boasting a choice of bars and dining options. On-site amenities include a swimming pool, and a children's club (5-14 years) is organised in peak season. Chichester is an attractive city, with its 12th century cathedral of particular interest. The city is also home to the Festival Theatre, one of England's flagship cultural centres. Bognor Regis was originally a smuggling village but it became popular as a holiday resort in the 19th century.

Facilities: Bar. Restaurant. Entertainment complex. Supermarket. Swimming pool. Fishing. Children's play area. Children's club. Tourist information. Mobile homes for rent (no touring pitches). Off site: Nearby resort of Bognor Regis (good selection of cafés, restaurants and shops). Walking and cycle routes. Chichester (cathedral city).

Open: 1 March - 31 October.

Directions: From Chichester take the A27 towards Havant and Brighton. At the Bognor Road roundabout take the fourth exit onto Vinnetrow Road (Pagham), and you will reach the site. GPS: 50.823885, -0.75119

Charges guide

Per unit incl. 2 persons and electricity	£ 9,00 - £ 24,00

Special offers
Prices are from £2 per night per dog.

You might like to know
Most dogs are welcome on our parks with a maximum of 2 dogs per booking. Some breeds of dog, including those listed in the Dangerous Dogs Act 1991, are not allowed.

☑ **Dogs welcome** *(subject to conditions)*
☑ **Dogs welcome all season**
☐ **Dogs welcome part season**
☑ **Breed restrictions**
  (e.g. only small dogs accepted)
☑ **Number restrictions** *(max. 1 or 2 dogs)*
☑ **Dog sanitary facilities**
  (e.g. waste bins, bags)
☐ **Dog showers**
☑ **On-site dog walking area**
☐ **Kennels**
☑ **Vet nearby**
  (able to help with UK Pet Passports)

Rivendale Caravan & Leisure Park

Buxton Road, Alsop-en-le-Dale, Ashbourne DE6 1QU (Derbyshire)
t: **01335 310311** e: **enquiries@rivendalecaravanpark.co.uk**
alanrogers.com/UK3850 www.rivendalecaravanpark.co.uk

Accommodation: ☑Pitch ☑Mobile home/chalet ☑Hotel/B&B ☐ Apartment

This unusual park has been developed in the bowl of a hill quarry which was last worked over 50 years ago. The steep quarry walls shelter three sides with marvellous views over the Peak National Park countryside to the south. A wide access road passes the renovated stone building which houses reception, a shop, bar and a café/restaurant. It gently climbs to a horseshoe shaped area providing 136 pitches, some of which are rather small, but most are of a generous size, with 16A electricity. The pitches are a mixture of hardstanding and grass, and are divided by shrubs. A further open, marked grass area is accessed by hardcore roads. All the pitches are within easy reach of the central stone-built toilet block which is in keeping with the environment and thoughtfully provided with underfloor heating. The park takes up about 11 acres and a further 26 acres belong to the owners with certain parts suitable for walking – a must to appreciate the Derbyshire countryside with its dry stone walls, wild flowers and a little more of the quarry history.

You might like to know
There is a network of footpaths directly accessible from the campsite ideal for exercising dogs. Well behaved dogs are allowed in the bar.

☑ **Dogs welcome** (subject to conditions)
☑ **Dogs welcome all season**
☐ **Dogs welcome part season**
☐ **Breed restrictions**
   (e.g. only small dogs accepted)
☑ **Number restrictions** (max. 1 or 2 dogs)
☐ **Dog sanitary facilities**
   (e.g. waste bins, bags)
☐ **Dog showers**
☐ **On-site dog walking area**
☐ **Kennels**
☐ **Vet nearby**
   (able to help with UK Pet Passports)

Facilities: First rate toilet facilities include some washbasins in cubicles for ladies, and an excellent en-suite room for disabled visitors. Laundry room. Shop (all essentials). Bar (evenings) and café with home-made and local food (open mornings, lunch and evenings, both with limited opening in low season). Packed lunches from reception. Special events monthly and games in main season. Hot tubs for hire, delivered to your pitch. WiFi. For rent on the park are 4 B&B rooms, a luxury caravan holiday home and a yurt (6 persons). Off site: Bicycle hire and riding 5 miles. Sailing and boat launching 8 miles. Fishing and golf 10 miles.

Open: All year excl. 9 January - 2 February.

Directions: Park is 7 miles north of Ashbourne on the A515 to Buxton, on the eastern side of the road. It is well signed between the turnings east to Alsop Moor and Matlock (A5012), but take care as this is a very fast section of the A515. GPS: 53.106383, -1.760567

Charges guide

Per unit incl. 2 persons and electricity	£ 14,50 - £ 19,00
extra person	£ 2,50
child (4-15 yrs)	£ 2,00
dog	£ 1,00

Croft Farm Water & Leisure Park

Bredon's Hardwick, Tewkesbury GL20 7EE (Gloucestershire)
t: 01684 772321 e: enquiries@croftfarmleisure.co.uk
alanrogers.com/UK4150 www.croftfarmleisure.co.uk

Accommodation: ☑Pitch ☑Mobile home/chalet ☐ Hotel/B&B ☐ Apartment

Croft Farm is an AALA licensed Watersports Centre with Royal Yachting Association approved tuition available for windsurfing, sailing, kayaking and canoeing. The lakeside campsite has around 96 level pitches, with electric hook-ups (10A), but there are many seasonal units, leaving around 36 pitches for tourists, plus some tent pitches. There are 36 gravel hardstandings with very little shade or shelter. 'Gym and Tonic' is a fully equipped gymnasium with qualified instructors, sunbed and sauna. Sports massage, aromatherapy and beauty treatments are available by appointment. Activity holidays for families and groups are organised. Campers can use their own non-powered boats on the lake with reduced launching fees and there is river fishing. There are plans to include a launch ramp onto the river. Climb Bredon Hill (2 miles) for a panoramic view of the Severn and Avon Valleys. Places of interest include Bredon Barn, pottery and church, and the historic town of Tewkesbury with its Abbey, theatre and indoor swimming pool.

You might like to know
The site is situated around a lake where there is a meandering footpath through the meadows that leads to the river Avon - good for exercising dogs.

☑ **Dogs welcome** *(subject to conditions)*

☑ **Dogs welcome all season**

☐ **Dogs welcome part season**

☐ **Breed restrictions**
(e.g. only small dogs accepted)

☑ **Number restrictions** *(max. 1 or 2 dogs)*

☐ **Dog sanitary facilities**
(e.g. waste bins, bags)

☐ **Dog showers**

☐ **On-site dog walking area**

☐ **Kennels**

☐ **Vet nearby**
(able to help with UK Pet Passports)

Facilities: A recently modernised building has excellent facilities with spacious hot showers, plus some dishwashing sinks. A heated unit in the main building is always open and best for cooler months; this provides further WCs, washbasins and showers, laundry and facilities for disabled campers. Gas. Cafe/bar (Fri-Sun low season, daily at other times). Takeaway. Gym. Playground. River fishing. Barrier and toilet block key (£5 deposit). Fenced dog exercise area. WiFi in the clubhouse (free to visitors spending £5 or over). Off site: Pub opposite. Tewkesbury 1.5 miles. Golf 3 miles. Riding 8 miles.

Open: 1 March - 31 December.

Directions: Bredon's Hardwick is midway between Tewkesbury and Bredon on B4080. Site entrance opposite 'Cross Keys Inn'. From M5 exit 9 take A438 (Tewkesbury), at first lights turn right into Shannon Way. Turn right at next lights, into Northway Lane, cross motorway bridge. Turn left into housing estate and cross second bridge. At T-junction turn right on B4080, site is on left. GPS: 52.015967, -2.130267

Charges guide

Per unit incl. 2 persons, electricity and awning	£ 16,00
extra person (over 3 yrs)	£ 3,50
dog	£ 1,00

Fforest Fields Caravan Park

Hundred House, Builth Wells LD1 5RT (Powys)
t: **01982 570406** e: **office@fforestfields.co.uk**
alanrogers.com/UK6320 www.fforestfields.co.uk

Accommodation: ☑Pitch ☑Mobile home/chalet ☐ Hotel/B&B ☐ Apartment

This secluded 'different' park is set on a family hill farm in the heart of Radnorshire. Truly rural, there are glorious views and a distinctly family atmosphere. This is simple country camping and caravanning at its best, without man-made distractions or intrusions. The facilities include 80 large pitches on level grass on a spacious and peaceful, carefully landscaped field by a stream. Electrical connections (mostly 16A) are available and there are 17 hardstanding pitches, also with electricity. Several additional areas without electricity are provided for tents. There are two new lakes, one for boating and fly fishing, the other for coarse fishing. A new reception and toilet block are planned. George and Kate, the enthusiastic owners, have opened up much of the farm for moderate or ample woodland and moorland trails which can be enjoyed with much wildlife to see. Indeed, wildlife is actively encouraged with nesting boxes for owls, songbirds and bats, by leaving field margins wild to encourage small mammals and by yearly tree planting.

You might like to know

This is a dog friendly site and there are plenty of lovely farm and woodland walks straight off the site, so dog walking is a real pleasure.

☑ **Dogs welcome** *(subject to conditions)*
☑ **Dogs welcome all season**
☐ **Dogs welcome part season**
☐ **Breed restrictions**
　(e.g. only small dogs accepted)
☑ **Number restrictions** *(max. 1 or 2 dogs)*
☐ **Dog sanitary facilities**
　(e.g. waste bins, bags)
☐ **Dog showers**
☑ **On-site dog walking area**
☐ **Kennels**
☐ **Vet nearby**
　(able to help with UK Pet Passports)

Facilities: The toilet facilities are acceptable with baby bath, dishwashing and laundry facilities including washing machines and a dryer. Milk, eggs, orange juice and gas are sold in reception, otherwise there are few on-site facilities. The village of Hundred House, 1 mile away, has a pub. Fishing. Torches are useful. Off site: Bicycle hire and golf 5 miles. Riding 10 miles.

Open: Easter - 17 November.

Directions: Park is 4 miles east of Builth Wells near the village of Hundred House on the A481. Follow brown signs. GPS: 52.17121, -3.31621

Charges guide

Per person	£ 3,50
child	£ 2,50
pitch	£ 4,50
electricity	£ 2,50
dog	free

Special low season rates for senior citizens. No credit cards.

UNITED KINGDOM – Pitlochry
Tummel Valley Holiday Park

Tummel Bridge, Pitlochry PH16 5SA (Perth and Kinross)
t: **01882 634221** e: **enquiries@parkdeanholidays.co.uk**
alanrogers.com/UK7305 www.parkdeanholidays.co.uk

Accommodation: ☑Pitch ☑Mobile home/chalet ☐ Hotel/B&B ☐ Apartment

Set in the Tay Forest Park on the banks of the River Tummel, this large family holiday park is part of the Parkdean Group. Divided into two areas by the roadway, the main emphasis is on chalets to let on the side that overlooks the river. Privately owned caravan holiday homes and touring pitches are on the other, quieter side. The 26 touring pitches, open plan with hardstanding, electricity hook-up and a shared water point, overlook a small fishing lake which is an added attraction for all the family. On arrival, you should turn right and park, then cross back to book in. The leisure complex with indoor and outdoor activities is on the river side, as is the reception office.

You might like to know
This site is set in a woodland park on the banks of River Tummel in the heart of the Tay Forest making it ideal for tranquil walks. Dogs are welcome in some of the holiday homes.

☑ **Dogs welcome** *(subject to conditions)*
☑ **Dogs welcome all season**
☐ **Dogs welcome part season**
☐ **Breed restrictions**
  (e.g. only small dogs accepted)
☑ **Number restrictions** *(max. 1 or 2 dogs)*
☐ **Dog sanitary facilities**
  (e.g. waste bins, bags)
☐ **Dog showers**
☐ **On-site dog walking area**
☐ **Kennels**
☐ **Vet nearby**
  (able to help with UK Pet Passports)

Facilities: The very clean toilet block has vanity style washbasins, pre-set showers and a bathroom in each section. Good facilities for disabled visitors. Well equipped laundry. Chemical disposal but no motorcaravan service point. Shop. Riverside entertainment complex with bar and terrace, restaurant and takeaway. Indoor heated pool and toddlers' splash pool. Solarium and sauna. Amusements. Separate area with pool tables. All weather sports court. Adventure play area. Crazy golf. Nature trails. Bicycle hire. Fishing. Note: all venues are non-smoking. Max. 2 dogs per unit. Off site: Golf and riding 10 miles. Buses leave near park entrance.

Open: 24 March - 1 November.

Directions: Travel through Pitlochry. After 2 miles turn left on B8019 to Tummel Bridge (10 miles). Park is on both the left and right. Tourers should turn right and park, then return to reception on the left. GPS: 56.70742, -4.02002

Charges guide

Per unit incl. 4 persons and electricity	£ 13,00 - £ 32,00
dog	£ 2,00 - £ 3,00

90

Forest Holidays Glenmore

Aviemore PH22 1QU (Highland)
t: **01479 861271**   e: **info@forestholidays.co.uk**
alanrogers.com/UK7680 www.forestholidays.co.uk

Accommodation: ☑Pitch ☑Mobile home/chalet ☐ Hotel/B&B ☐ Apartment

Forest Holidays is a partnership between the Forestry Commission and The Camping and Caravanning Club. This site is attractively laid out in a fairly informal style in several adjoining areas connected by narrow part gravel, part tarmac roads, with access to the lochside. One of these areas, the Pinewood Area, is very popular and has 32 hardstandings (some distance from the toilet block). Of the 260 marked pitches on fairly level, firm grass, 122 have electricity (16A). This site with something for everyone would be great for family holidays. The Glenmore Forest Park lies close to the sandy shore of Loch Morlich amidst conifer woods and surrounded on three sides by the impressive Cairngorm mountains. It is conveniently situated for a range of activities, including skiing (extensive lift system), orienteering, hill and mountain walking (way-marked walks), fishing (trout and pike) and non-motorized watersports on the Loch.

You might like to know
This site occupies an idyllic location beside the sandy beach at Loch Morlich, in the Cairngorms National Park - many great walks in the area.

☑ **Dogs welcome** *(subject to conditions)*
☑ **Dogs welcome all season**
☐ **Dogs welcome part season**
☐ **Breed restrictions**
   (e.g. only small dogs accepted)
☑ **Number restrictions** *(max. 1 or 2 dogs)*
☐ **Dog sanitary facilities**
   (e.g. waste bins, bags)
☐ **Dog showers**
☐ **On-site dog walking area**
☐ **Kennels**
☐ **Vet nearby**
   (able to help with UK Pet Passports)

Facilities: New toilet and shower blocks. Next to the site is a range of amenities including a well stocked shop (open all year), a café serving a variety of meals and snacks, and a Forestry Commission visitor centre and souvenir shop. Barbecues are not permitted in dry weather. Sandy beach. Off site: The Aviemore centre with a wide range of indoor and outdoor recreation activities including skiing 7 miles. Golf within 15 miles. Fishing and boat trips.

Open: All year.

Directions: Immediately south of Aviemore on B9152 (not A9 bypass) take B970 then follow sign for Cairngorm and Loch Morlich. Site entrance is on right past the loch.
GPS: 57.167033, -3.694717

Charges guide

Per unit incl. 2 persons	£ 11,00 - £ 25,50
extra person	£ 5,25 - £ 8,25
child	£ 2,75 - £ 4,25

Discounts for families, disabled guests and senior citizens.

Glen Nevis Caravan Park

Glen Nevis, Fort William PH33 6SX (Highland)
t: **01397 702191** e: **camping@glen-nevis.co.uk**
alanrogers.com/7UK830 www.glen-nevis.co.uk

Accommodation: ☑Pitch ☑Mobile home/chalet ☐Hotel/B&B ☐Apartment

Just outside Fort William in a most attractive and quiet situation with views of Ben Nevis, this spacious park is used by those on active pursuits as well as sightseeing tourists. It comprises eight quite spacious fields, divided between caravans, motorcaravans and tents (steel pegs required). It is licensed for 250 touring caravans but with no specific tent limits. The large touring pitches, many with hardstanding, are marked with wooden fence dividers, 174 with electricity (13A) and 100 also have water and drainage. The park becomes full in the peak months but there are vacancies each day. If reception is closed (possible in low season) you site yourself. There are regular security patrols at night in busy periods. The park's own restaurant and bar with good value bar meals is a short stroll from the park, open to all. A well managed park with bustling, but pleasing ambience, watched over by Ben Nevis. Around 1,000 acres of the Glen Nevis estate are open to campers to see the wildlife and explore this lovely area.

You might like to know
The site is set in 34 acres of magnificent tree-clad countryside which is ideal for walking dogs. There is no charge for dogs on the camping pitches.

- ☑ **Dogs welcome** *(subject to conditions)*
- ☑ **Dogs welcome all season**
- ☐ **Dogs welcome part season**
- ☐ **Breed restrictions**
  (e.g. only small dogs accepted)
- ☑ **Number restrictions** *(max. 1 or 2 dogs)*
- ☐ **Dog sanitary facilities**
  (e.g. waste bins, bags)
- ☐ **Dog showers**
- ☐ **On-site dog walking area**
- ☐ **Kennels**
- ☐ **Vet nearby**
  (able to help with UK Pet Passports)

Facilities: The four modern toilet blocks with showers (extra showers in two blocks); and units for visitors with disabilities. An excellent block in Nevis Park (one of the eight camping fields) has some washbasins in cubicles, showers, further facilities for disabled visitors, a second large laundry room and dishwashing sinks. Motorcaravan service point. Shop (Easter-mid Oct), barbecue area and snack bar (May-mid Sept). Play area on bark. Off site: Pony trekking, golf and fishing near.

Open: 15 March - 31 October.

Directions: Turn off A82 to east at roundabout just north of Fort William following camp sign. GPS: 56.804517, -5.073917

Charges guide

Per person	£ 1,60 - £ 2,50
child (5-15 yrs)	£ 0,80 - £ 1,30
pitch incl. awning	£ 4,40 - £ 12,00
serviced pitch plus	£ 2,00 - £ 3,00

Blackwater Valley Caravan Park

Mallow-Killarney Road, Fermoy (Co. Cork)
t: 025 321 47
alanrogers.com/IR9470

Accommodation: ☑Pitch ☑Mobile home/chalet ☐ Hotel/B&B ☐ Apartment

The location of this park provides the best of both worlds, as it backs onto green fields adjacent to the Blackwater river, yet is within 200 metres of Fermoy town. Pat and Nora Ryan live overlooking the park which ensures supervision and attention to detail. Ideal for touring, there are 25 pitches with hardstanding and electricity connections (13A) and water supply nearby, and considerable additional space for tents towards the rear of the park. There are five caravan holiday homes to rent. Fermoy provides local amenities, such as a cinema and the town park with a leisure centre with pool and a play area. There are restaurants and pubs, many providing traditional music. The Mitchelstown Caves, Mount Mellary, Lismore Castle and many other attractions are within easy reach of the park.

You might like to know
This site can be found on the banks of the River Blackwater, just 200 m. from the town of Fermoy.

☑ **Dogs welcome** (subject to conditions)
☑ **Dogs welcome all season**
☐ **Dogs welcome part season**
☐ **Breed restrictions**
   (e.g. only small dogs accepted)
☑ **Number restrictions** (max. 1 or 2 dogs)
☐ **Dog sanitary facilities**
   (e.g. waste bins, bags)
☐ **Dog showers**
☐ **On-site dog walking area**
☐ **Kennels**
☐ **Vet nearby**
   (able to help with UK Pet Passports)

Facilities: Modern, tiled toilet block provides the usual facilities including for disabled visitors. Laundry room with ironing facilities. Campers' kitchen with cooking facilities and dining area. TV and games room. Motorcaravan service point. Off site: Fishing adjacent to park. Bicycle hire 500 m. Golf 3.5 km. Beach 35 km. Internet access 100 m. Petrol station with gas across the road.

Open: 15 March - 31 October.

Directions: In Fermoy town take the N72 for Mallow. Park is 200 m. from the junction. GPS: 52.141498, -8.281873

Charges guide

Per unit incl. 2 persons and electricity	€ 24,00
extra person	€ 6,00
child	€ 3,00

No credit cards.

IRELAND – Killarney

Fleming's White Bridge

Ballycasheen Road, Killarney (Co. Kerry)
t: 064 663 1590   e: info@killarneycamping.com
alanrogers.com/IR9620   www.killarneycamping.com

Accommodation: ☑Pitch ☑Mobile home/chalet ☐ Hotel/B&B ☐ Apartment

Once past the county border, the main road from Cork to Killarney (N22) runs down the valley of the Flesk river. On the final approach to Killarney off the N22 Cork road, the river veers away from the road to enter the Lower Lake. On this prime rural position, between the road and the river, and within comfortable walking distance of the town, is Fleming's White Bridge, a nine acre woodland park. The ground is flat, landscaped and generously adorned with flowers, shrubs and trees. There are 92 pitches (46 caravans and 46 tents) that extend beyond a wooden bridge to an area surrounded by mature trees. A new toilet block, one of three, is sited in this area. This is obviously a park of which the owners are very proud, and the family personally supervise the reception and grounds, maintaining high standards of hygiene, cleanliness and tidiness. The park's location so close to Ireland's premier tourism centre makes this park an ideal base to explore Killarney and the southwest.

You might like to know

Dogs are welcome here but are not allowed in mobile homes.

☑ **Dogs welcome** (subject to conditions)

☑ **Dogs welcome all season**

☐ **Dogs welcome part season**

☐ **Breed restrictions**
  (e.g. only small dogs accepted)

☑ **Number restrictions** (max. 1 or 2 dogs)

☐ **Dog sanitary facilities**
  (e.g. waste bins, bags)

☐ **Dog showers**

☐ **On-site dog walking area**

☐ **Kennels**

☐ **Vet nearby**
  (able to help with UK Pet Passports)

Facilities: Three toilet blocks are maintained to high standards. Motorcaravan service point. Campers' drying room and two laundries. Shop (1/6-1/9). Two TV rooms and a games room. Fishing (advice and permits provided). Canoeing (own canoes). Bicycle hire. Woodland walks. Off site: Riding 3 km. Golf 2 km.

Open: 9 April - 5 October, 23-26 October.

Directions: From Cork and Mallow: at N72/N22 junction continue towards Killarney and take first turn left (signed Ballycasheen Road). Proceed for 300 m. to archway entrance on left. From Limerick: follow N22 Cork road. Pass Super Valu and The Heights Hotel take first right (signed Ballycasheen Road) and continue as above. From Kenmare: On N71, pass Gleneagles Hotel and Flesk Bridge. Turn right at traffic lights into Woodlawn Road and Ballycasheen Road and continue 2 km. to archway.
GPS: 52.05595, -9.47458

Charges guide

Per unit incl. 2 persons and electricity	€ 30,00 - € 31,00
extra person	€ 8,00
child	€ 3,00 - € 11,00

No credit cards.

BELGIUM – Gierle

Camping De Lilse Bergen

Strandweg 6, Gierle, B-2275 Lille (Antwerp)
t: 014 557 901 e: info@lilsebergen.be
alanrogers.com/BE0655 www.lilsebergen.be

Accommodation: ☑Pitch ☑Mobile home/chalet ☐Hotel/B&B ☐Apartment

This attractive, quietly located holiday site has 485 shady pitches, of which 239 (all with 10A electricity) are for touring units. Set on sandy soil among rhododendrons and pine trees and arranged around a large lake, the site has a Mediterranean feel. It is well fenced, with a night guard and comprehensive, well labelled, fire fighting equipment. Cars are parked away from units. The site is really child-friendly with each access road labelled with a different animal symbol to enable children to find their own unit easily. An entertainment programme is organised in high season. The lake has marked swimming and diving areas (for adults), a sandy beach, an area for watersports, plus a separate children's pool complex (depth 50 cm) with a most imaginative playground. There are lifeguards and the water meets 'Blue Flag' standards. A building by the lake houses changing rooms, extra toilets, showers and a baby room. There are picnic areas and lakeside or woodland walks.

You might like to know
There are some great walks near the site, around the lake or through the woods.

☑ **Dogs welcome** *(subject to conditions)*
☑ **Dogs welcome all season**
☐ **Dogs welcome part season**
☐ **Breed restrictions**
   (e.g. only small dogs accepted)
☑ **Number restrictions** *(max. 1 or 2 dogs)*
☐ **Dog sanitary facilities**
   (e.g. waste bins, bags)
☐ **Dog showers**
☐ **On-site dog walking area**
☐ **Kennels**
☑ **Vet nearby**
   (able to help with UK Pet Passports)

Facilities: Five of the six main toilet blocks have been fully refitted to a good standard (a new one was added in 2010) and can be heated. Some washbasins in cubicles and good hot showers (on payment). Well equipped baby rooms. Facilities for disabled campers. Laundry. Barrier keys can be charged up with units for operating showers, washing machine etc. First aid post. Motorcaravan service point. Restaurant (all year, weekends only in winter), takeaway and well stocked shop (Easter-30/9; weekends only outside July/Aug). Tennis. Minigolf. Boules. Climbing wall. New playground, trampolines and skateboard ramp. Pedaloes, kayaks and bicycles for hire. Children's electric cars and pedal kart tracks (charged for). Off site: Golf 1 km.

Open: All year.

Directions: From E34 Antwerp-Eindhoven take exit 22. On the roundabout take the exit for 'Lilse Bergen' and follow forest road to site entrance. GPS: 51.28908, 4.85508

Charges guide

Per unit incl. 4 persons and electricity	€ 20,00 - € 26,50
dog	€ 4,50

Ardennen Camping Bertrix

Route de Mortehan, B-6880 Bertrix (Luxembourg)
t: 061 412 281 e: info@campingbertrix.be
alanrogers.com/BE0711 www.campingbertrix.be

Accommodation: ☑Pitch ☑Mobile home/chalet ☐ Hotel/B&B ☐ Apartment

Bertrix is located at the heart of the Belgian Ardennes, between the towns of Bastogne and Bouillon and overlooking the hills of the Semois valley. The 498 pitches are terraced, giving an open aspect and views for everyone. The 303 level touring pitches all have electricity and are near amenities. The activities, particularly for children, are of a high standard and well supervised, plus many guided walks allow guests to wonder at the natural beauty of the area with its fabulous panoramic views. A visit to the nearby ruined castle at Bouillon is a must, as well as tasting the many Belgian beers. The war Memorial and excellent museum at Bastogne commemorate the Battle of the Bulge. If you have never visited the Ardennes before, this site is a good introduction; wooded hills, valleys and rivers (used for canoeing) are all around. The town of Bertrix is unusual with all its buildings roofed in slate and many walls also, this includes the church with its spire and one large wall all covered in this local material. The mine itself is worth a visit.

You might like to know

A maximum of one pet is permitted per unit of rented accommodation.

- ☑ **Dogs welcome** (subject to conditions)
- ☑ **Dogs welcome all season**
- ☐ **Dogs welcome part season**
- ☐ **Breed restrictions**
  (e.g. only small dogs accepted)
- ☑ **Number restrictions** (max. 1 or 2 dogs)
- ☐ **Dog sanitary facilities**
  (e.g. waste bins, bags)
- ☐ **Dog showers**
- ☐ **On-site dog walking area**
- ☐ **Kennels**
- ☐ **Vet nearby**
  (able to help with UK Pet Passports)

Facilities: Five well appointed toilet blocks, one with facilities for disabled visitors. The central one has a large laundry and a special, brightly decorated unit for children, with basins, toilets, showers of varying heights and baby baths in cubicles. Motorcaravan service point. Shop for basics and bread. Excellent restaurant and bar (closed in low season on Tuesday and Thursday), with satellite TV and internet access and a terrace overlooking pool. Large heated swimming and paddling pools (supervised high season). Tennis. Bicycle hire. Children's games room. Ardennes chalets and holiday homes for rent. Off site: Canoeing. Fishing. Walking and cycle trails. Shops, banks and restaurants in Bertrix.

Open: 1 April - 14 November.

Directions: Take exit 25 from the E411 motorway and join the N89 towards Bertrix. After 6.5 km. join the N884 to Bertrix and upon arrival in the town, follow yellow signs to site. GPS: 49.83861, 5.25122

Charges guide

Per unit incl. 2 persons	€ 16,00 - € 28,00
extra person (over 2 yrs)	€ 4,00 - € 5,50
electricity (10A)	€ 3,50

LUXEMBOURG – Obereisenbach

Camping Kohnenhof

Maison 1, L-9838 Obereisenbach
t: **929 464** e: **kohnenhof@pt.lu**
alanrogers.com/LU7680 www.campingkohnenhof.lu

Accommodation: ☑Pitch ☑Mobile home/chalet ☐ Hotel/B&B ☐ Apartment

Nestling in a valley with the River Our running through it, Camping Kohnenhof offers a very agreeable location for a relaxing family holiday. From the minute you stop at the reception you are assured of a warm and friendly welcome. Numerous paths cross through the wooded hillside so this could be a haven for walkers. A little wooden ferry crosses the small river across the border to Germany. The river is shallow and safe for children (parental supervision essential). A large sports field and play area with a selection of equipment caters for younger campers. During the high season, an entertainment programme is organised for parents and children. The owner organises special golf weeks with games on different courses (contact the site for details). The restaurant is part of an old farmhouse and, with its open fire to keep it warm, offers a wonderful ambience to enjoy a meal. Discounts have been agreed at several local golf courses.

Special offers
Special rental accommodation (mobile homes and cabins) for families with dogs.

You might like to know
Dogs are allowed in the restaurant and may swim in the kilometre-long stretch of river that runs through the campsite. Many hiking trips start straight from the site.

☑ **Dogs welcome** *(subject to conditions)*
☑ **Dogs welcome all season**
☐ **Dogs welcome part season**
☐ **Breed restrictions**
    (e.g. only small dogs accepted)
☐ **Number restrictions** *(max. 1 or 2 dogs)*
☑ **Dog sanitary facilities**
    (e.g. waste bins, bags)
☐ **Dog showers**
☑ **On-site dog walking area**
☐ **Kennels**
☑ **Vet nearby**
    (able to help with UK Pet Passports)

Facilities: Heated sanitary block with showers and washbasins in cabins. Motorcaravan service point. Laundry. Bar, restaurant, takeaway. Games and TV room. Baker calls daily. Sports field with play equipment. Boules. Bicycle hire. Golf weeks. Discounts on six local 18-hole golf courses. WiFi. Off site: Bus to Clervaux and Vianden stops (4 times daily) outside site entrance. Riding 5 km. Castle at Vianden 14 km. Monastery at Clervaux 14 km. Golf 15 km.

Open: 15 March - 10 November.

Directions: Take N7 north from Diekirch. At Hosingen, turn right onto the narrow and winding CR324 signed Eisenbach. Follow site signs from Eisenbach or Obereisenbach.
GPS: 50.01602, 6.13600

Charges guide

Per unit incl. 2 persons and electricity	€ 19,90 - € 28,00
extra person	€ 4,00
dog	€ 3,00

.

Camping De Molenhoek

Molenweg 69a, NL-4493 NC Kamperland (Zeeland)
t: **0113 371 202** e: info@molenhoek.com
alanrogers.com/NL5570 www.demolenhoek.com

Accommodation: ☑Pitch ☑Mobile home/chalet ☐ Hotel/B&B ☐ Apartment

This family-run site makes a pleasant contrast to the livelier coastal sites in this popular holiday area. It is rurally situated 3 km. from the Veerse Meer, which is very popular for all sorts of watersports. Catering for 300 permanent or seasonal holiday caravans and 100 touring units, it is neat, tidy and relatively spacious. The marked touring pitches are divided into small groups with surrounding hedges and trees giving privacy and some shade, and electrical connections are available. A large outdoor pool is Molenhoek's latest attraction. Entertainment is organised in season (dance evenings, bingo, etc.) as well as a disco for youngsters. Although the site is quietly situated, there are many excursion possibilities in the area including the towns of Middelburg, Veere and Goes and the Delta Expo exhibition.

You might like to know

A completely renovated swimming pool was opened here in May 2010.

- ☑ **Dogs welcome** *(subject to conditions)*
- ☑ **Dogs welcome all season**
- ☐ **Dogs welcome part season**
- ☐ **Breed restrictions**
  (e.g. only small dogs accepted)
- ☑ **Number restrictions** *(max. 1 or 2 dogs)*
- ☐ **Dog sanitary facilities**
  (e.g. waste bins, bags)
- ☐ **Dog showers**
- ☐ **On-site dog walking area**
- ☐ **Kennels**
- ☐ **Vet nearby**
  (able to help with UK Pet Passports)

Facilities: Sanitary facilities in one fully refurbished and one newer block, include some washbasins in cabins. Toilet and shower facilities for disabled visitors and for babies. Laundry facilities. Motorcaravan services. Simple bar/restaurant with terrace and TV room. Restaurant/bar. Swimming pool (15/5-15/9). Playground. Bicycle hire. Off site: Tennis and watersports close. Riding 1 km. Shop 2 km. Fishing 2.5 km.

Open: 1 April - 28 October.

Directions: Site is west of the village of Kamperland on the 'island' of Noord Beveland. From the N256 Goes - Zierikzee road, exit west onto the N255 Kamperland road. Site is signed south of this road. GPS: 51.57840, 3.69642

Charges guide

Per unit incl. 2 or 3 persons and electricity	€ 21,00 - € 33,50
extra person	€ 3,50 - € 4,50
dog	€ 2,50 - € 3,00

No credit cards.

NETHERLANDS – Wolphaartsdijk

Camping De Veerhoeve

Veerweg 48, NL-4471 NC Wolphaartsdijk (Zeeland)
t: **0113 581 155** e: **info@deveerhoeve.nl**
alanrogers.com/NL5580 www.deveerhoeve.nl

Accommodation: ☑Pitch ☑Mobile home/chalet ☐Hotel/B&B ☐Apartment

This is a family-run site near the shores of the Veerse Meer which is ideal for family holidays. It is situated in a popular area for watersports and is well suited for sailing, windsurfing or fishing enthusiasts, with boat launching 100 m. away. A sandy beach and recreation area ideal for children is only a five minute walk. As with most sites in this area, there are many mature, static and seasonal pitches. However, part of the friendly, relaxed site is reserved for touring units with 90 marked pitches on grassy ground, all with electrical connections. A member of the Holland Tulip Parcs group.

Facilities: Sanitary facilities in three blocks have been well modernised with full tiling. Hot showers are on payment. Laundry facilities. Motorcaravan services. Supermarket (all season). Restaurant and snack bar. TV room. Tennis. Playground and play field. Games room. Bicycle hire. Fishing. Accommodation for groups. Only one dog is accepted. WiFi. Off site: Slipway for launching boats 100 m. Riding 2 km. Golf 5 km.

Open: 1 April - 30 October.

Directions: From N256 Goes - Zierikzee road take Wolphaartsdijk exit. Follow through village and signs to site (be aware - one of the site signs is obscured by other road signs and could be missed). GPS: 51.54678, 3.81345

Charges guide

Per unit incl. 1-4 persons	€ 21,50 - € 24,50
incl. electricity (6A), water and drainage	€ 22,50 - € 25,50
incl. TV connection	€ 24,00 - € 27,50

You might like to know

The Veerse Meer is a well known holiday area. Surfing, sailing, swimming and angling are all popular here. There are several wooded recreation areas nearby, which are ideal for a relaxing dog walk.

☑ **Dogs welcome** *(subject to conditions)*
☑ **Dogs welcome all season**
☐ **Dogs welcome part season**
☐ **Breed restrictions**
  (e.g. only small dogs accepted)
☑ **Number restrictions** *(max. 1 or 2 dogs)*
☐ **Dog sanitary facilities**
  (e.g. waste bins, bags)
☐ **Dog showers**
☐ **On-site dog walking area**
☐ **Kennels**
☐ **Vet nearby**
  (able to help with UK Pet Passports)

NETHERLANDS – Leeuwarden

Camping De Kleine Wielen

Groene Ster 14, NL-8926 XE Leeuwarden (Friesland)
t: 0511 431 660 e: info@dekleinewielen.nl
alanrogers.com/NL5750 www.dekleinewielen.nl

Accommodation: ☑Pitch ☑Mobile home/chalet ☐ Hotel/B&B ☐ Apartment

Camping De Kleine Wielen (small wheels) is named after a small lake of the same name that lies in the 1,000 ha nature and recreation area of 'De Groene Ster'. The campsite is adjacent to the lake – possible activities include boating in the lake or cycling and walking around this beautiful area of forest, grassland and ponds. The site provides 480 pitches, of which 150 are for touring units. The remaining pitches are used for privately owned mobile homes. All the touring pitches have 4A electricity and many have wonderful views over the water and surrounding countryside. The position of the site next to the water (the lake is not fenced) opens up many opportunities for sailing, rowing, canoeing or windsurfing. You can follow the river leading from the lake by boat, or on shore by bicycle or car as it leads through the villages and towns such as Hindeloopen, Stavoren and Dokkum. With its central Friesland location, De Kleine Wielen is ideal for a taste of the real 'Friesland' culture and is definitely worth visiting.

Facilities: Four toilet blocks provide washbasins in cabins and preset showers (coin operated). Maintenance is variable. Facilities for disabled visitors. Motorcaravan service point. Shop (1/5-30/9). Café/restaurant and snack bar (1/4-30/9). Playground. Sports pitch. Minigolf. Lake with beach. Fishing. Rowing boats. Surf boards. Extensive recreation programme in July/Aug. Off site: Golf 1 km. Boat launching 2 km. Riding 5 km.

Open: 1 April - 30 September.

Directions: From the N355 turn off east towards Leeuwarden and follow campsite signs.
GPS: 53.21650, 5.88703

Charges guide

Per person	€ 3,95
child (2-12 yrs)	€ 2,95
pitch incl. car	€ 7,25
electricity (4A)	€ 3,25

You might like to know
This site is located within a 1,000-acre nature park – some wonderful dog walking opportunities here!

☑ **Dogs welcome** (subject to conditions)

☑ **Dogs welcome all season**

☐ **Dogs welcome part season**

☐ **Breed restrictions**
  (e.g. only small dogs accepted)

☑ **Number restrictions** (max. 1 or 2 dogs)

☐ **Dog sanitary facilities**
  (e.g. waste bins, bags)

☐ **Dog showers**

☐ **On-site dog walking area**

☐ **Kennels**

☐ **Vet nearby**
  (able to help with UK Pet Passports)

Camping De Zanding

Vijverlaan 1, NL-6731 CK Otterlo (Gelderland)
t: 0318 596 111 e: info@zanding.nl
alanrogers.com/NL5780 www.vakantieparkdezanding.nl

Accommodation: ☑Pitch ☑Mobile home/chalet ☐Hotel/B&B ☐Apartment

De Zanding is a family run, highly rated site that offers almost every recreational facility, either on site or nearby, that active families or couples might seek. Immediately after the entrance, a lake is to the left where you can swim, fish, sunbathe or try a two-person canoe. There are many sporting options and organised high season programmes for all ages. There are 463 touring pitches spread around the site (all with 4/6/10A electricity), some individual and separated, others in more open spaces shaded by trees. Some serviced pitches are in small groups between long stay units and there is another area for tents. Seasonal units and mobile homes take a further 508 pitches. Minutes away is the Hoge Veluwe National Park, recommended for a great day out either cycling, walking or visiting the Kröller-Müller Museum (with the second largest collection of Van Gogh paintings after Amsterdam). In the village of Otterlo are a 14th century Dutch Reformed Church and the Netherlands Tile Museum. A member of the Holland Tulip Parcs group.

Facilities: First class sanitary facilities are housed in five modern blocks that are clean, well maintained and well equipped. Good provision for babies and visitors with disabilities. Laundry. Kitchen. Motorcaravan services. Gas supplies. Supermarket. Restaurant/bar (30/3-28/10). Lake swimming. Fishing. Tennis. Minigolf. Boules. Five play areas. Bicycle hire. Organised activities.

Open: 3 April - 31 October.

Directions: Leave A12 Utrecht - Arnhem motorway at Oosterbeek at exit 25 and join the N310 to Otterlo. Then follow camping signs to site, watching carefully for entrance. GPS: 52.09310, 5.77757

Charges guide

Per unit incl. 2 persons and electricity	€ 21,00 - € 32,90
extra person	€ 4,70
dog	€ 3,75

You might like to know
Don't miss the Kröller-Müller museum, one of the world's finest collections of Van Gogh paintings.

☑ **Dogs welcome** (subject to conditions)

☑ **Dogs welcome all season**

☐ Dogs welcome part season

☐ **Breed restrictions**
  (e.g. only small dogs accepted)

☑ **Number restrictions** (max. 1 or 2 dogs)

☐ **Dog sanitary facilities**
  (e.g. waste bins, bags)

☐ **Dog showers**

☐ **On-site dog walking area**

☐ **Kennels**

☐ **Vet nearby**
  (able to help with UK Pet Passports)

NETHERLANDS – Harlingen

Camping De Zeehoeve

Westerzeedijk 45, NL-8862 PK Harlingen (Friesland)
t: 0517 413 465   e: info@zeehoeve.nl
alanrogers.com/NL6080   www.zeehoeve.nl

Accommodation: ☑Pitch ☑Mobile home/chalet ☐ Hotel/B&B ☐ Apartment

Superbly located, directly behind the sea dyke of the Waddensea and just a kilometre from the harbour of Harlingen, De Zeehoeve is an attractive and spacious site. It has 300 pitches (125 for tourers), all with 10A electricity and 20 with water, drainage and electricity. There are 16 hardstandings for motorcaravans and larger units. Some pitches have views over the Harlingen canal where one can moor small boats. An ideal site for rest and relaxation, for watersports or to visit the attractions of Harlingen and Friesland. After a day of activity, one can wine and dine in the site restaurant or at one of the many pubs in the town. This splendid location allows one the opportunity to watch the sun slowly setting from the sea dyke. You can also stroll through Harlingen or take the ferry to Vlieland or Terschelling. It is possible to moor boats at Harlingen, or to hire a boat or book an organised sailing or sea fishing trip.

You might like to know
This site is well placed for visits to the islands of Terschelling or Vlieland.

☑ **Dogs welcome** *(subject to conditions)*

☑ **Dogs welcome all season**

☐ **Dogs welcome part season**

☐ **Breed restrictions**
(e.g. only small dogs accepted)

☑ **Number restrictions** *(max. 1 or 2 dogs)*

☐ **Dog sanitary facilities**
(e.g. waste bins, bags)

☐ **Dog showers**

☐ **On-site dog walking area**

☐ **Kennels**

☐ **Vet nearby**
(able to help with UK Pet Passports)

Facilities: Hikers' cabins and boarding houses. Three sanitary blocks include open style washbasins with cold water only, washbasins in cabins with hot and cold water, controllable showers (on payment). Family showers and baby bath. Facilities for disabled campers. Cooking hob. Launderette. Motorcaravan services. Bar/restaurant (1/7-31/8). WiFi (charged). Play area. Bicycle hire. Boat launching. Pedalo and canoe hire. Fishing. Extensive entertainment programme in July/Aug. Off site: Beach 200 m. Riding 10 km.

Open: 1 April - 15 October.

Directions: From Leeuwarden take the A31 southwest to Harlingen, then follow site signs. GPS: 53.16237, 5.41688

Charges guide

Per unit incl. 2 persons and electricity	€ 17,10 - € 20,60
extra person	€ 4,05
child (4-11 yrs)	€ 3,55
tent (no car) incl. 2 persons	€ 15,10
pet	€ 3,00

Recreatiegebied Erkemederstrand

Erkemederweg 79, NL-3896 LB Zeewolde (Flevoland)
t: **0365 228 421** e: **info@erkemederstrand.nl**
alanrogers.com/NL6200 www.erkemederstrand.nl

Accommodation: ☑Pitch ☑Mobile home/chalet ☐Hotel/B&B ☐Apartment

The Erkemederstrand (the beach of Erkemede) is a leisure park at Flevoland, with direct access to the Nuldernauw, a sandy beach, water and forest. It provides a campsite for families, a marina, an area for youngsters to camp, a camping area for groups and a recreation area for day visitors. The campsite itself is divided into two areas: one before the dyke at the waterfront and one behind the dyke. The pitches are spacious (around 125 m²) and all have electricity, water and drainage. The focal point of the site and marina is the beach restaurant, 'De Jutter'. This restaurant offers a varied menu for more formal dining as well as catering for snacks, takeaway, ice creams or a cold beer on the terrace. There is plenty to do on the campsite, including a Red Indian village for children where they can build huts, a children's farm and an extended programme of animation. Obviously with the proximity of the lake there are many opportunities for watersports.

You might like to know
The only real 'dog camp' in the Netherlands! All your dogs, whether there are one, two or ten of them, are welcome anywhere. With numerous facilities for your four-legged friends. There is a 1.5 km. dog beach where dogs can run free throughout the year, a dog shower, a dog bar at the restaurant, a dog sitting service and dog training.

- ☑ **Dogs welcome** *(subject to conditions)*
- ☑ **Dogs welcome all season**
- ☐ **Dogs welcome part season**
- ☐ **Breed restrictions**
  (e.g. only small dogs accepted)
- ☐ **Number restrictions** *(max. 1 or 2 dogs)*
- ☑ **Dog sanitary facilities**
  (e.g. waste bins, bags)
- ☑ **Dog showers**
- ☑ **On-site dog walking area**
- ☑ **Kennels**
- ☑ **Vet nearby**
  (able to help with UK Pet Passports)

Facilities: Four neat and clean toilet blocks (access by key, exclusively for campers). Washbasins in cabins, showers and family bathrooms (free hot water). Dishwashing and laundry facilities in heated buildings. Shop for basic provisions. Bar, restaurant and takeaway. Several play areas and children's farm. Watersports facilities and lake swimming. Football pitch. Minigolf. Bicycle hire. Extended animation programme. Off site: Golf and riding 11 km.

Open: 20 March - 25 October.

Directions: From the A28 (Utrecht - Zwolle) take exit 9 (Nijkerk/Almere) and follow N301 to Zeewolde. Cross the bridge and turn right following signs to site. From Amsterdam/Almere, take exit 5 and follow N27 to Zeewolde; this road changes into the N305. Then take N301 to Nijkerk. At the bridge turn right and follow signs to site. GPS: 52.27021, 5.48871

Charges guide

Per unit incl. 2 persons and electricity	€ 22,50 - € 28,50
extra person	€ 2,50
dog	€ 2,00

Camping BreeBronne

Lange Heide 9, NL-5993 PB Maasbree (Limburg)
t: 0774 652 360 e: info@breebronne.nl
alanrogers.com/NL6520 www.breebronne.nl

Accommodation: ☑Pitch ☑Mobile home/chalet ☐Hotel/B&B ☐Apartment

One of the top campsites in the Netherlands, BreeBronne is set around a large lake in a forest region. There are 370 pitches, of which 220 are for touring units. These are at least 100 m² in size and all have electricity (10A), water, waste water and cable TV connections. The touring pitches are placed in separate areas from the static units and some pitch areas are kept for people without dogs. The lake provides a sandy beach with a water slide and opportunities for swimming, sailing and windsurfing. Alternatively, you can swim in the heated open air pool or the sub-tropical, heated indoor pool with its special children's area. Possible excursions from the site might include a visit to Arcen, beside the Maas river, with its Schloss garden and the nearby naturally heated thermal bath. There are boat trips on the Maas. Shopping in Venlo is good with its Saturday morning market. Member of Leading Campings Group.

You might like to know
Lovely hiking trails from this site lead you along the Maas, the Peel and through countless delightful villages.

☑ **Dogs welcome** *(subject to conditions)*
☑ **Dogs welcome all season**
☐ **Dogs welcome part season**
☐ **Breed restrictions**
  (e.g. only small dogs accepted)
☑ **Number restrictions** *(max. 1 or 2 dogs)*
☐ **Dog sanitary facilities**
  (e.g. waste bins, bags)
☐ **Dog showers**
☐ **On-site dog walking area**
☐ **Kennels**
☐ **Vet nearby**
  (able to help with UK Pet Passports)

Facilities: The sanitary facilities are top class with a special section for children, decorated in fairy tale style, and excellent provision for disabled visitors and seniors. Launderette. Dog shower. Solarium. Private bathrooms for hire. Shop (1/4-31/10). Bar and 'De Bron' restaurant with regional specialities (all year). Takeaway. Outdoor swimming pool (15/5-1/10). Indoor pool with area for children (all year). Play area. Play room. Internet. Tennis. Animation. Fishing. Bicycle hire. Max. 1 dog. Off site: Fishing 2 km. Golf and riding 5 km. Walking in the National Parks.

Open: All year.

Directions: BreeBronne is 8 km. west of Venlo. From autobahn A67 towards Eindhoven take exit 38 and head south on the 277 road. After 3 km. fork right for Maasbree, then left (Maasbree) on the 275. At roundabout in Maasbree take third exit (site signed). Go through town and turn right after 2 km. to site 1 km. on left.
GPS: 51.36665, 6.04166

Charges guide

Per unit incl. 4 persons	€ 28,50 - € 46,60
extra person	€ 4,90
dog	€ 5,50
private bathroom	€ 12,00

DENMARK – Hampen

Hampen Sø Camping

Hovedgaden 31, DK-7362 Hampen (Vejle)
t: 75 77 52 55   e: info@hampen-soe-camping.dk
alanrogers.com/DK2044   www.hampencamping.dk

Accommodation: ☑Pitch ☑Mobile home/chalet ☐Hotel/B&B ☐Apartment

If you are heading north towards Denmark to cross to Norway or Sweden, then this site in a natural setting close to lakes and moors could be a useful stopover. There are 230 pitches in total, with 80 seasonal units plus 34 cabins, but there will always be space for touring units. The pitches are arranged in large grassy bays taking around 15 units, and there are 10A electric hook-ups (some long leads may be needed). The nearby Hampen See lake is a pleasant walk through the forest and is said to be one of the cleanest lakes for swimming in Denmark. Many people stay here to visit Legoland, the Lion Park and Silkeborg, in addition to walking and cycling in this pleasant area. English is spoken.

You might like to know
Pitches here are all 100 m², flat and with electricity (10A). The site motto is 'Camping as on a golf course', with regular checks on the ground to ensure that the grass always looks its best.

☑ **Dogs welcome** *(subject to conditions)*
☑ **Dogs welcome all season**
☐ **Dogs welcome part season**
☐ **Breed restrictions**
   (e.g. only small dogs accepted)
☑ **Number restrictions** *(max. 1 or 2 dogs)*
☐ **Dog sanitary facilities**
   (e.g. waste bins, bags)
☐ **Dog showers**
☐ **On-site dog walking area**
☐ **Kennels**
☐ **Vet nearby**
   (able to help with UK Pet Passports)

Facilities: Three toilet blocks, one basic near the entrance, one central on the site with new laundry, new children's room and new kitchen, and one to far end with two family shower rooms. En-suite facilities for disabled visitors. Laundry. Good supermarket and restaurant open all year (weekends in winter) and to the general public. Takeaway. Kitchen. Games and TV rooms. Small outdoor pool (15/6-1/9). Covered minigolf. Trampolines and new play equipment. Race track for mini cars. WiFi. Off site: Riding 500 m. Fishing 3 km. Golf 18 km.

Open: All year.

Directions: Site lies on road no.176, 500 m. southwest of its junction with road no.13 between Vejle and Viborg (around 50 km. south of Viborg). Look for Spar supermarket and camping signs. GPS: 56.01425, 9.36427

Charges guide

Per person	€ 8,97
child (0-11 yrs)	€ 4,83
electricity	€ 3,86
dog	€ 1,38

No credit cards.

Bøsøre Strand Feriepark

Bøsørevej 16, DK-5874 Hesselager (Fyn)
t: **62 25 11 45** e: **info@bosore.dk**
alanrogers.com/DK2210 www.bosore.dk

Accommodation: ☑Pitch ☑Mobile home/chalet ☐ Hotel/B&B ☐ Apartment

A themed holiday site on the eastern coast of Fyn, the tales of Hans Christian Andersen are evident in the design of the indoor pool complex and the main outdoor play area here. The former has two pools on different levels, two hot tubs and a sauna and features characters from the stories; the latter has a fairytale castle with a moat as its centrepiece. There are 300 pitches in total, and with only 25 seasonal units there should always be room for touring units out of the main season. All have 10A electricity, there are 124 multi-serviced pitches and 20 hardstandings. In common with several other sites in Denmark, Bøsøre operates a card system which allows use of the facilities (showers, sauna, solarium, washing machine etc). You only pay for what you have used when you leave. The card also operates the barriers and opens doors to other facilities.

You might like to know

Occasional dog shows are organised here, in a special area. For several years, these have included bulldogs, Berne Enners and Schapendoes.

☑ **Dogs welcome** (subject to conditions)
☑ **Dogs welcome all season**
☐ **Dogs welcome part season**
☐ **Breed restrictions**
  (e.g. only small dogs accepted)
☑ **Number restrictions** (max. 1 or 2 dogs)
☐ **Dog sanitary facilities**
  (e.g. waste bins, bags)
☐ **Dog showers**
☐ **On-site dog walking area**
☐ **Kennels**
☐ **Vet nearby**
  (able to help with UK Pet Passports)

Facilities: Sanitary facilities are in one main central block and a smaller unit close to reception. They provide all the usual facilities plus some family bathrooms, special children's section, baby rooms, facilities for disabled visitors. They could be stretched in high season. Laundry. Motorcaravan service point. Shop, bar/restaurant, pizzeria, takeaway (all open all season). Kitchen (water charged). Solarium. Indoor pool complex. Games and TV rooms. Playground with moat. Animal farm. Internet access and WiFi. Bicycle hire. Entertainment (main season). Boat launching with jetty.
Off site: Golf 20 km.

Open: Easter - 22 October.

Directions: Site is on the coast about midway between Nyborg and Svendborg. From road no. 163 just north of Hesselager, turn towards coast signed Bøsøre Strand (5 km).
GPS: 55.19287, 10.80530

Charges guide

Per person	DKK 64
child (0-11 yrs)	DKK 43
pitch	DKK 25 - 70
electricity	DKK 28

TopCamp Feddet

Feddet 12, DK-4640 Faxe (Sjælland)
t: **56 72 52 06** e: **info@feddetcamping.dk**
alanrogers.com/DK2255 www.feddetcamping.dk

Accommodation: ☑Pitch ☑Mobile home/chalet ☐ Hotel/B&B ☐ Apartment

This interesting, spacious site with ecological principles is located on the Baltic coast. It has a fine, white, sandy beach (Blue Flag) which runs the full length of one side, with the Præstø fjord on the opposite side of the peninsula. There are 413 pitches for touring units, generally on sandy grass, with mature pine trees giving adequate shade. All have 10A electricity and 20 are fully serviced (water, electricity, drainage and sewage). Two recently constructed sanitary buildings, which have been specially designed, are clad with larch panels from sustainable local trees and are insulated with flax mats. They have natural ventilation, with ventilators controlled by sensors for heat, humidity and smell. All this saves power and provides a comfortable climate inside. Heating, by a wood chip furnace (backed up by a rapeseed oil furnace), is CO_2 neutral and replaces 40,000 litres of heating oil annually. Taps are turned off automatically, and lighting is by low wattage bulbs with PIR switching. Recycling is also very important here.

You might like to know
Dogs are allowed in a number of the campsite chalets.

☑ **Dogs welcome** *(subject to conditions)*
☑ **Dogs welcome all season**
☐ **Dogs welcome part season**
☐ **Breed restrictions**
   (e.g. only small dogs accepted)
☑ **Number restrictions** *(max. 1 or 2 dogs)*
☐ **Dog sanitary facilities**
   (e.g. waste bins, bags)
☐ **Dog showers**
☐ **On-site dog walking area**
☐ **Kennels**
☐ **Vet nearby**
   (able to help with UK Pet Passports)

Facilities: Both sanitary buildings are impressive, equipped to a very high standard. Family bathrooms (with twin showers), complete suites for small children and babies. Facilities for disabled visitors. Laundry. Kitchens, dining room and TV lounge. Excellent motorcaravan service point. Well stocked licensed shop. Licensed bistro and takeaway (1/5-20/10 but weekends only outside peak season). Minigolf. Games room. Indoor playroom and several playgrounds for all ages. Event camp for children. Pet zoo. WiFi. Massage. Watersports. Fishing.
Off site: Abseiling, pool. Amusement park.

Open: All year.

Directions: From south on E47/55 take exit 38 towards Præsto. Turn north on 209 road towards Fakse and from Vindbyholt follow site signs. From the north on E47/55 take exit 37 east towards Fakse. Just before Fakse turn south on 209 road and from Vindbyholt, site signs. GPS: 55.17497, 12.10203

Charges guide

Per unit incl. 2 persons and electricity	DKK 250 - 323
extra person	DKK 72
child (0-11 yrs)	DKK 50 - 105
dog	DKK 20

Lærdal Ferie & Fritidspark

Grandavegens, N-6886 Lærdal (Sogn og Fjordane)

t: **57 66 66 95** e: **info@laerdalferiepark.com**

alanrogers.com/NO2375 www.laerdalferiepark.com

Accommodation: ☑Pitch ☑Mobile home/chalet ☑Hotel/B&B ☑Apartment

This site is beside the famous Sognefjord, the longest fjord in the world. It is ideally situated if you want to explore the glaciers, fjords and waterfalls of the region. The 100 pitches are level with well trimmed grass and connected by tarmac roads and are suitable for tents, caravans and motorcaravans. There are 80 electrical hook-ups. The fully licensed restaurant serves traditional meals as well as snacks and pizzas. The pretty little village of Lærdal, only 400 m. away, is well worth a visit. A walk among the old, small wooden houses is a pleasant and interesting experience. You can hire boats on the site for short trips on the fjord. Guided hiking, cycling and fishing trips are also available. The site also provides cabins, flats and rooms to rent, plus a brand new motel, all very modern and extremely tastefully designed.

You might like to know

Dogs are welcome on site but are not allowed in the chalets.

☑ **Dogs welcome** *(subject to conditions)*

☑ **Dogs welcome all season**

☐ **Dogs welcome part season**

☐ **Breed restrictions**
   (e.g. only small dogs accepted)

☑ **Number restrictions** *(max. 1 or 2 dogs)*

☐ **Dog sanitary facilities**
   (e.g. waste bins, bags)

☐ **Dog showers**

☐ **On-site dog walking area**

☐ **Kennels**

☐ **Vet nearby**
   (able to help with UK Pet Passports)

Facilities: Two modern and well decorated sanitary blocks with washbasins (some in cubicles), showers on payment, and toilets. Facilities for disabled visitors. Children's room. Washing machine and dryer. Kitchen. Motorcaravan services. Small shop. Bar, restaurant and takeaway (20/5-5/9). TV room. Playground. Motorboats, rowing boats, canoes, bicycles and pedal cars for hire. Bicycle hire. Fishing. Internet (WiFi) at reception.
Off site: Cruises on the Sognefjord 400 m. The Norwegian Wild Salmon Centre 400 m. Riding 500 m. Golf 12 km. The Flåm railway 40 km.

Open: All year,
by telephone request 1 Nov - 14 March.

Directions: Site is on road 5 (from the Oslo - Bergen road, E 16) 400 m. north of Lærdal village centre. GPS: 61.09977, 7.46962

Charges guide

Per unit incl. 2 persons and electricity	NOK 210
extra person	NOK 50
child (4-15 yrs)	NOK 25

GERMANY – Waldfischbach-Burgalben

Camping Clausensee

D-67714 Waldfischbach-Burgalben (Rhineland Palatinate)
t: 063 335 744 e: info@campingclausensee.de
alanrogers.com/DE3259 www.campingclausensee.de

Accommodation: ☑Pitch ☑Mobile home/chalet ☐ Hotel/B&B ☐ Apartment

Clausensee is a well equipped family site on the banks of an attractive lake with a wide grassy bank. This site is open all year. Pitches are grassy with varying degrees of shade. Most pitches have electricity. A number of special motorcravan pitches are provided and a discounted overnight rate is available (arrivals after 19.00 and departures before 10.00). A number of fully equipped chalets, caravans and bungalow tents are available for rent. The lake is the focal point of the site with pedaloes and rowing boats for hire. It is also popular with fishermen (permit required – available on site). Clausensee lies at the heart of the Pfälzerwald (Palatinate Forest), a vast area of natural beauty, and one of the biggest forests in Europe. The German wine route extends along the eastern side of the forest, bordering the Upper Rhine Valley. The Vosges mountains in France rise to the south. This is excellent cycling and walking country with hundreds of kilometres of waymarked trails. The Mountainbike Park Pfälzerwald was added in 2005.

You might like to know
There are some wonderful hiking trails in the region, so you can explore the beautiful scenery along the Rhine.

☑ **Dogs welcome** (subject to conditions)
☑ **Dogs welcome all season**
☐ **Dogs welcome part season**
☐ **Breed restrictions**
   (e.g. only small dogs accepted)
☑ **Number restrictions** (max. 1 or 2 dogs)
☐ **Dog sanitary facilities**
   (e.g. waste bins, bags)
☐ **Dog showers**
☐ **On-site dog walking area**
☐ **Kennels**
☐ **Vet nearby**
   (able to help with UK Pet Passports)

Facilities: Shop. Bar. Restaurant. Takeaway meals. Direct access to lake (suitable for swimming). Pedaloes and rowing boats. Fishing. Bicycle hire. Play area. Tourist information. Caravans, equipped tents and chalets for rent. Off site: Golf (discounts available for campers). Walking and cycling. German wine route.

Open: All year.

Directions: Approaching from the A6 Kaiserslautern-Mannheim, motorway, leave at exit 15 (Kaiserslautern-West) and join B270 towards Waldfischbach-Burgalben. From Waldfischbach-Burgalben follow signs to the site for 7 km. (towards Clausen). GPS: 49.27544, 7.720116

Charges guide

Per unit incl. 2 persons and electricity	€ 22,50 - € 25,50
extra person	€ 7,00
child (under 13 yrs)	€ 3,70
dog	€ 4,20

Camping & Ferienpark Teichmann

Zum Träumen 1A, D-34516 Vöhl-Herzhausen (Hessen)
t: 056 352 45 e: info@camping-teichmann.de
alanrogers.com/DE3280 www.camping-teichmann.de

Accommodation: ☑Pitch ☑Mobile home/chalet ☐Hotel/B&B ☐Apartment

Situated near the eastern end of the 27 km. long Edersee and the National Park Kellerwald-Edersee, this attractively set site is surrounded by wooded hills and encircles a six-hectare lake, which has separate areas for swimming, fishing and boating. Of the 460 pitches, 250 are touring, all with 10A electricity and 50 with fresh and waste water connections. The pitches are on level grass, some having an area of hardstanding, and are separated by hedges and mature trees. At the far side of the lake from the entrance is a separate area for tents with its own sanitary block. The adjoining national park, a popular leisure region, offers a wealth of holiday/sporting activities including walking, cycling, (there are two passenger ferries that take cycles) boat trips, cable car and much more, full details are available at the friendly reception. For winter sport lovers, the ski centre at Winterberg is only 30 km. away from this all year round site. With a wide range of facilities for children this is an ideal family site as well as being suited to country lovers who can enjoy the endless forest and lakeside walks/cycle tracks in the park.

You might like to know

There are some excellent walking areas within the immediate vicinity of the site, including the Kellerwald Edersee National Park.

☑ **Dogs welcome** *(subject to conditions)*

☑ **Dogs welcome all season**

☐ **Dogs welcome part season**

☐ **Breed restrictions**
(e.g. only small dogs accepted)

☑ **Number restrictions** *(max. 1 or 2 dogs)*

☐ **Dog sanitary facilities**
(e.g. waste bins, bags)

☐ **Dog showers**

☐ **On-site dog walking area**

☐ **Kennels**

☐ **Vet nearby**
(able to help with UK Pet Passports)

Facilities: Three good quality sanitary blocks can be heated and have free showers, washbasins (open and in cabins), baby rooms and facilities for wheelchair users. Laundry. Motorcaravan services. Café and shop (both summer only). Restaurant by entrance open all day (closed Feb). Watersports. Boat and bicycle hire. Lake swimming. Fishing. Minigolf. Tennis. Playground. Sauna. Solarium. Disco (high season). Internet access. Off site: New National Park opposite site entrance. Riding 500 m. Golf 25 km. Cable car (you can take bikes). Aquapark. Boat trips on the Edersee.

Open: All year.

Directions: Site is 45 km. from Kassel. From A44 Oberhausen - Kassel autobahn, take exit 64 for Diemelstadt and head south for Korbach. Site is between Korbach and Frankenberg on the B252 road, 1 km. to the south of Herzhausen at the pedestrian traffic lights. GPS: 51.17550, 8.89067

Charges guide

Per unit incl. 2 persons and electricity	€ 25,00 - € 29,00

GERMANY – Neuenburg

Gugel's Dreiländer Camping

Oberer Wald 3, D-79395 Neuenburg-am-Rhein (Baden-Württemberg)
t: 076 317 719   e: info@camping-gugel.de
alanrogers.com/DE3455   www.camping-gugel.de

Accommodation: ☑Pitch ☑Mobile home/chalet ☐ Hotel/B&B ☐ Apartment

Set in natural heath and woodland, Gugel's is an attractive site with 220 touring pitches, either in small clearings in the trees, in open areas or on a hardstanding section used for single night stays. All have electricity (16A), and some also have water, waste water and satellite TV connections. Opposite is a meadow where late arrivals and early departures may spend the night. There may be some road noise near the entrance. The site may become very busy in high season and at Bank Holidays, but you should always find room. The excellent pool and wellness complex add to the attraction of this all year site. There is a social room with satellite TV where guests are welcomed with a glass of wine and a slide presentation of the attractions of the area. The Rhine is within walking distance. Neuenburg is ideally placed, not only for enjoying and exploring the south of the Black Forest, but also for night stops when travelling from Frankfurt to Basel on the A5 autobahn. The permanent caravans set away from the tourist area, with their well tended gardens, enhance rather than detract from the natural beauty.

You might like to know
This site, apart from from having green and wooded areas, is also situated at the start of the Nordic Walking course.

☑ **Dogs welcome** (subject to conditions)
☑ **Dogs welcome all season**
☐ **Dogs welcome part season**
☐ **Breed restrictions**
    (e.g. only small dogs accepted)
☑ **Number restrictions** (max. 1 or 2 dogs)
☐ **Dog sanitary facilities**
    (e.g. waste bins, bags)
☐ **Dog showers**
☐ **On-site dog walking area**
☐ **Kennels**
☐ **Vet nearby**
    (able to help with UK Pet Passports)

Facilities: Three good quality heated sanitary blocks include some washbasins in cabins. Baby room. Facilities for disabled visitors. Laundry facilities. Motorcaravan services. Shop. Excellent restaurant. Takeaway (weekends and daily in high season). Wellness centre. Indoor/outdoor pool. Boules. Tennis. Fishing. Minigolf. Barbecue. Beach bar. Bicycle hire. Community room with TV. Activity programme (high season). Play areas. Off site: Riding 1.5 km. Golf 5 km. Neuenburg, Breisach, Freiburg, Basel and the Black Forest.

Open: All year.

Directions: From autobahn A5 take Neuenburg exit, turn left, then almost immediately left at traffic lights, left at next junction and follow signs for 2 km. to site (called 'Neuenburg' on most signs). GPS: 47.79693, 7.55000

Charges guide

Per unit incl. 2 persons and electricity	€ 22,00 - € 26,50
extra person	€ 6,50
child (2-15 yrs)	€ 3,00
dog	€ 3,00

Camping Elbsee

Am Elbsee 3, D-87648 Aitrang (Bavaria (S))
t: 083 432 48   e: camping@elbsee.de
alanrogers.com/DE3672   www.elbsee.de

Accommodation: ☑Pitch ☑Mobile home/chalet ☑Hotel/B&B ☐ Apartment

This attractive site, with its associated hotel and restaurant about 400 m. away, lies on land sloping down to a lake. This is not an area well known to tourists, although the towns of Marktoberdorf (14 km), Kaufbeuren (16 km) and Kempten (21 km) merit a visit. With this in mind, the owners have set about providing good facilities and a developing program of activities. All the 120 touring pitches have access to electricity (16A) and 78 also have their own water supply and waste water outlet. Some of the pitches (those restricted to tents) slope slightly. In high season there are organised outings, musical performances on site or at the hotel, painting courses and activities for children. Next to the site is a supervised lake bathing area, operated by the municipality, with a kiosk selling drinks and snacks, a playground and an indoor play area. Entrance to this is at a reduced price for campers.

You might like to know
This site is in an area of meadows and forests and near to an interconnected network of hiking trails through the alps.

- ☑ **Dogs welcome** *(subject to conditions)*
- ☑ **Dogs welcome all season**
- ☐ **Dogs welcome part season**
- ☐ **Breed restrictions**
  (e.g. only small dogs accepted)
- ☑ **Number restrictions** *(max. 1 or 2 dogs)*
- ☐ **Dog sanitary facilities**
  (e.g. waste bins, bags)
- ☐ **Dog showers**
- ☐ **On-site dog walking area**
- ☐ **Kennels**
- ☐ **Vet nearby**
  (able to help with UK Pet Passports)

Facilities: Two clean, well appointed heated sanitary blocks include free showers and washbasins, all in cabins, a children's bathroom and family bathrooms to rent. Facilities for disabled visitors. Dog shower. Motorcaravan service point. Shop (order bread for following day). New playground, indoor play area and activity rooms. TV, games and meeting rooms. Sports field. Fishing. Bicycle hire. Riding. Boat launching. Activity programme (20/7-31/8). Off site: At hotel, very good restaurant, takeaway and bar. Shop and ATM point 2 km. Golf 12 km.

Open: All year.

Directions: From centre of Marktoberdorf, take minor road northwest to Ruderatshofen and from there take minor road west towards Aitrang. Just south of Aitrang, site is signed to south of the road. The road to the site (2 km) is winding and narrow, but two caravans can just about pass. GPS: 47.80277, 10.55343

Charges guide

Per unit incl. 2 persons and electricity (per kWh)	€ 21,90 - € 24,00
extra person	€ 6,20
child (4-15 yrs)	€ 3,00
dog	€ 4,00

Kur-Gutshof-Camping Arterhof

Hauptstrasse 3, Lengham, D-84364 Bad Birnbach (Bavaria (S))
t: 085 639 6130 e: info@arterhof.de
alanrogers.com/DE3696 www.arterhof.de

Accommodation: ☑Pitch ☑Mobile home/chalet ☑Hotel/B&B ☐ Apartment

Arterhof is a high quality site which forms part of a broader holiday complex in Bavaria's southeast corner, within easy access of Passau and Salzburg. There are 200 pitches here, a number of which are occupied by mobile homes (available for rent). Pitches are of a good size and are all equipped with electricity and WiFi. A very wide range of amenities is on offer, including smart, modern toilet blocks with underfloor heating, a golf practice green and a Kneipp spa treatment area. An entire health suite is available as part of the Arterhof complex, which also includes hotel accommodation. A convivial bar/restaurant has been developed in a former stable block and now specialises in local delicacies such as Ripperlessen. The farm shop also offers a wide array of local produce, including smoked cheeses. Sports amenities include a covered pool, Finnish sauna and steam room. The surrounding Rottal valley offers numerous sporting activities including a number of golf courses, Nordic walking, and even parachuting. Regular excursions are organised to Passau, Salzburg and the Bavarian forests.

You might like to know

As well as an extensive spa and swimming complex this site has an outdoor swimming lake. Trail maps are available from reception to explore the area by foot.

☑ **Dogs welcome** *(subject to conditions)*

☑ **Dogs welcome all season**

☐ **Dogs welcome part season**

☐ **Breed restrictions**
  (e.g. only small dogs accepted)

☑ **Number restrictions** *(max. 1 or 2 dogs)*

☐ **Dog sanitary facilities**
  (e.g. waste bins, bags)

☐ **Dog showers**

☐ **On-site dog walking area**

☐ **Kennels**

☐ **Vet nearby**
  (able to help with UK Pet Passports)

Facilities: Shop. Bar. Restaurant and takeaway. Covered swimming pool. Health suite. Sauna. Steam room. Play area. Children's zoo. Games room. Tourist information. Mobile homes for rent. Off site: Hiking and cycle tracks. Riding. Golf. Ballooning. Parachuting.

Open: All year.

Directions: Site is close to the town of Bad Birnbach. Approaching from the north (Regensburg), leave the A3 autobahn at exit 06 and head south on B20 to Eggenfelden. Then, head east on B388, bypassing Pfarrkirchen and, on reaching Bad Birnbach, follow local signs to the site. GPS: 48.435176, 13.109415

Charges guide

Per unit incl. 2 persons and electricity (plus meter)	€ 21,90
extra person	€ 6,30
child (2-14 yrs)	€ 3,50
dog	€ 2,50

GERMANY – Bad Griesbach

Kur & Feriencamping Dreiquellenbad

Singham 40, D-94086 Bad Griesbach (Bavaria (S))
t: 085 329 6130   e: info@camping-bad-griesbach.de
alanrogers.com/DE3697   www.camping-bad-griesbach.de

Accommodation: ☑Pitch ☑Mobile home/chalet ☐ Hotel/B&B ☐ Apartment

This site is to the southwest of Passau, a town which dates back to Roman times and lies on a peninsula between the rivers Danube and Inn. Dreiquellenbad is an exceptional site in a quiet rural area, with 200 pitches, all of which are used for touring units. All pitches have electricity, water, waste water and TV points. English is spoken at reception which also houses a shop and good tourist information. A luxury leisure complex includes indoor and outdoor thermal pools, sauna, Turkish bath and jacuzzi (the use of which is free to campers). An adjoining building provides various beauty and complementary health treatments. A member of Leading Campings Group.

You might like to know

There are some excellent thermal spa and wellness facilities within easy walking distance of this site.

☑ **Dogs welcome** *(subject to conditions)*
☑ **Dogs welcome all season**
☐ **Dogs welcome part season**
☐ **Breed restrictions**
   (e.g. only small dogs accepted)
☑ **Number restrictions** *(max. 1 or 2 dogs)*
☐ **Dog sanitary facilities**
   (e.g. waste bins, bags)
☑ **Dog showers**
☐ **On-site dog walking area**
☐ **Kennels**
☐ **Vet nearby**
   (able to help with UK Pet Passports)

Facilities: Excellent sanitary facilities include private cabins and free showers, facilities for disabled visitors, special child facilities and a dog shower. Two private bathrooms for rent. Laundry facilities. Bar/restaurant. Motorcaravan services. Shop. Gym. Luxury leisure complex. Play area. Bicycle hire. Fishing. Internet. WiFi. Off site: Golf 2 km. Spa facilities of Bad Griesbach within walking distance.

Open: All year.

Directions: Site is 15 km. from the A3. Take exit 118 and follow signs for Pocking. After 2 km. turn right on B388. Site is in the hamlet of Singham - turn right into Karpfhan then left towards site. GPS: 48.42001, 13.19261

Charges guide

Per unit incl. 2 persons and electricity	€ 10,90 - € 11,90
extra person	€ 7,30
child (0-14 yrs)	€ 4,50
dog	€ 2,30

GERMANY – Userin

Camping Havelberge am Woblitzsee

An de Havelberg 1, D-17237 Userin/Ot Gross Quassau (Mecklenburg-West Pomerania)
t: **039 812 4790** e: **info@haveltourist.de**
alanrogers.com/DE3820 www.haveltourist.de

Accommodation: ☑Pitch ☑Mobile home/chalet ☐ Hotel/B&B ☐ Apartment

The Müritz National Park is a very large area of lakes and marshes, popular for birdwatching as well as watersports, and Havelberge is a large, well equipped site to use as a base for enjoying the area. It is quite steep in places with many terraces, most with shade, less in newer areas, with views over the lake. There are 400 pitches in total with 330 good sized, numbered touring pitches, most with 16A electrical connections, and 230 pitches on a newly developed area to the rear of the site with water and drainage. Pitches on the new field are level and separated by low hedges and bushes but have no shade. Over 170 seasonal pitches with a number of attractive chalets and an equal number of mobile homes in a separate area. In the high season this is a busy park with lots going on to entertain families of all ages, whilst in the low seasons this is a peaceful base for exploring an unspoilt area of nature.

Special offers
Free dog trainer with organised activities (agility training) on the sports field.

You might like to know
Dog swimming area in the lake. Waste bag stations on the site. Dog walks on the site (on lead) and in the forest. No fighting dogs accepted.

☑ **Dogs welcome** *(subject to conditions)*
☑ **Dogs welcome all season**
☐ **Dogs welcome part season**
☑ **Breed restrictions**
    (e.g. only small dogs accepted)
☑ **Number restrictions** *(max. 1 or 2 dogs)*
☑ **Dog sanitary facilities**
    (e.g. waste bins, bags)
☑ **Dog showers**
☑ **On-site dog walking area**
☐ **Kennels**
☑ **Vet nearby**
    (able to help with UK Pet Passports)

Facilities: Four sanitary buildings (one new and of a very high standard) provide very good facilities, with private cabins, showers on payment and large section for children. Fully equipped kitchen and laundry. Motorcaravan service point. Small shop and modern restaurant (April-Oct). The lake provides fishing, swimming from a small beach and boats can be launched (over 5 hp requires a German boat licence). Canoes, rowing boats, windsurfers and bikes can be hired. Play areas and entertainment in high season. Internet access. Off site: Riding 3.5 km.

Open: All year.

Directions: From A19 Rostock - Berlin road take exit 18 and follow B198 to Wesenberg and go left to Klein Quassow and follow site signs. GPS: 53.30517, 13.00133

Charges guide

Per unit incl. 2 persons and electricity	€ 15,30 - € 31,50
extra person	€ 4,00 - € 6,50
child (2-14 yrs)	€ 1,50 - € 4,30
dog	€ 1,00 - € 4,30

CZECH REPUBLIC – Vrchlabi

Holiday Park Lisci Farma

Dolni Branna 350, CZ-54362 Vrchlabi (Vychodocesky)
t: 499 421 473   e: info@liscifarma.cz
alanrogers.com/CZ4590   www.liscifarma.cz

Accommodation: ☑Pitch ☑Mobile home/chalet ☑Hotel/B&B ☐ Apartment

This is truly an excellent site that could be in Western Europe considering its amenities, pitches and welcome. However, Lisci Farma retains a pleasant Czech atmosphere. In the winter months, when local skiing is available, snow chains are essential. The 260 pitches are fairly flat, although the terrain is slightly sloping and some pitches are terraced. There is shade and some pitches have hardstanding. The site is well equipped for the whole family with its adventure playground offering trampolines for children, archery, beach volleyball, Russian bowling and an outdoor bowling court for older youngsters. A beautiful sandy, lakeside beach is 800 m. from the entrance. The more active amongst you can go paragliding or rock climbing, with experienced people to guide you. This site is very suitable for relaxing or exploring the culture of the area. Excursions to Prague are organised and, if all the sporting possibilities are not enough, the children can take part in the activities of the entertainment team, while you are walking or cycling or enjoying live music at the Fox Saloon.

You might like to know
This site is open all year – maybe a good choice for a winter break?

☑ **Dogs welcome** *(subject to conditions)*
☑ **Dogs welcome all season**
☐ **Dogs welcome part season**
☐ **Breed restrictions**
   (e.g. only small dogs accepted)
☑ **Number restrictions** *(max. 1 or 2 dogs)*
☐ **Dog sanitary facilities**
   (e.g. waste bins, bags)
☐ **Dog showers**
☐ **On-site dog walking area**
☐ **Kennels**
☐ **Vet nearby**
   (able to help with UK Pet Passports)

Facilities: Two good sanitary blocks, one new in 2005 near the entrance and another modern block next to the hotel, both include toilets, washbasins and spacious, controllable showers (on payment). Child size toilets and baby room. Toilet for disabled visitors. Sauna and massage. Launderette with sinks, hot water and a washing machine. Shop (15/6-15/9). Bar/snack bar with pool table. Games room. Swimming pool (6x12 m). Adventure style playground on grass with climbing wall. Trampolines. Tennis. Minigolf. Archery. Russian bowling. Paragliding. Rock climbing. Bicycle hire. Animation programme. Excursions to Prague. Off site: Fishing and beach 800 m. Riding 2 km. Golf 5 km.

Open: 1 December - 31 March and 1 May - 31 October.

Directions: Follow road no. 14 from Liberec to Vrchlabi. At the roundabout turn in the direction of Prague and site is about 1 mile on the right. GPS: 50.61036, 15.60264

Charges guide

Per unit incl. 2 persons and electricity	CZK 417 - 800
extra person	CZK 75 - 115
child (5-12 yrs)	CZK 59 - 90
dog	CZK 59 - 90

116

Camping Country

Hluboke Masuvky 257, CZ-67152 Hluboke Masuvky (Jihomoravsky)
t: 515 255 249 e: camping-country@cbox.cz
alanrogers.com/CZ4896 www.camp-country.com

Accommodation: ☑Pitch ☑Mobile home/chalet ☐Hotel/B&B ☐Apartment

Camping Country is a well cared for and attractively landscaped site, close to the historical town of Znojmo. It is a rural location close to a National Park and close to the Austrian border, which would make it ideal either as a stopover on your way south and for a longer stay to enjoy the new cycling routes which have been set out in the National Park. Camping Country has 60 pitches (all for tourers), 30 with 6A electricity, on two fields – one behind the main house taking 6 or 8 units, the other larger one with a gravel access road. The fields are connected by two wooden bridges (one is only fenced on one side). Varieties of low hedges and firs partly separate the pitches. To the front of the site is a paddock with two horses and facilities for minigolf, volleyball, basketball and tennis. In the garden of the main house is a paddling pool. Colourful flowers and trees give the site a pleasant atmosphere. We feel that Camping Country is certainly one of the better Czech sites.

You might like to know
As its name suggests, a great site for exploring the Czech countryside – maybe the National Nature Reserve at Podyjí, or castles in Vranov or Bítov.

☑ **Dogs welcome** *(subject to conditions)*

☑ **Dogs welcome all season**

☐ **Dogs welcome part season**

☐ **Breed restrictions**
(e.g. only small dogs accepted)

☑ **Number restrictions** *(max. 1 or 2 dogs)*

☐ **Dog sanitary facilities**
(e.g. waste bins, bags)

☐ **Dog showers**

☐ **On-site dog walking area**

☐ **Kennels**

☐ **Vet nearby**
(able to help with UK Pet Passports)

Facilities: Modern and comfortable toilet facilities provide British style toilets, open washbasins (cold water only) and free, controllable hot showers. Campers' kitchen. Bar/restaurant with one meal served daily. Play area. Tennis. Minigolf. Riding. Some live music nights in high season. Internet access. Tours to Vienna, Brno and wine cellars organised. Torch useful. Off site: Fishing, boat launching 2 km and beach 10 km.

Open: 1 May - 31 October.

Directions: Coming from the northwest on the E59 road exit to the east at Kasarna onto the 408 road and continue north on the 361 road towards Hluboké Masuvky. Site is well signed. GPS: 48.9192, 16.0256

Charges guide

Per unit incl. 2 persons and electricity	CZK 440 - 490
extra person	CZK 120
child (3-12 yrs)	CZK 60 - 170
dog	CZK 50

Been to any good campsites lately?
We have

You'll find them here...

The UK's market leading independent guides to the best campsites

...and, new for 2011, here...

101 great campsites, ideal for your specific hobby, pastime or passion

Want independent campsite reviews at your fingertips?

You'll find them here...

Over 3,000 in-depth campsite reviews at **www.alanrogers.com**

...and even here...

An exciting free app from iTunes and the Apple app store*

*available January 2011

Want to book your holiday on one of Europe's top campsites?

We can do it for you. No problem.

The best campsites in the most popular regions - we'll take care of everything

alan rogers travel

Discover the best campsites in Europe
with Alan Rogers

alanrogers.com
01580 214000

index

index

index